Human Rights and Insurgency

Human Rights and Insurgency

The North-East India

Editors
Ranju R. Dhamala
Sukalpa Bhattacharjee

SHIPRA

(2019, First Published in 2002)

Rs. 1250
ISBN: 978-81-938382-6-6

2026
PoD Impression

Human Rights and Insurgency

Published by:
SHIPRA PUBLICATIONS
LG 18-19, Pankaj Central Market,
I.P. Ext., Patparganj, Delhi 110092, India
11 47322068, 9650028065, 9810522367
info@shiprapublication.com
www.shiprapublication.com

Preface

The volume seeks to understand the issue of Human Rights and Insurgency in the North East from various standpoints. The common point in all these is the individual authors' attempt to examine and seek plausible solutions to the problem so that the average human subjects do not continue to suffer the trauma of torture, confinement and loss of freedom.

The objective of the publication of this book is to bring together diverse points of view on the burning issues affecting the North East (NE) India. Our sole endeavour has been to voice the opinion of people from different positions of the conflict centering around Insurgency and Human Rights and to proceed towards a dialogic encounter with each other. We would feel rewarded if this volume generates such a climate of dialogue in the region.

We thank all those persons and organisations who extended their support and cooperation in the venture. In particular, we would like to put on record our sincere thanks to the following persons:

Professor J.B. Bhattacharjee, former The Vice-Chancellor of Assam University and Faculty Members, Department of Political Science, Assam University, Silchar; Dr. D. Choudhury, Dr. B.S. Butola and other members of the Centre for Interdisciplinary Studies on North East India, Shillong; the Principal and Staff members of G.C. College, Silchar, Assam; staff members of Counter-Insurgency and Jungle Warfare School, Vairengte, Mizora; Mr. Natwarbhai Thakkar.

We must record our deep sense of appreciation to Professor Goutam Biswas, Mr. Rajesh Dev and Dr. Prasenjit Biswas, whose constant help, discussion, suggestions, and constructive criticism helped us finalize the manuscript. Thanks are also due to Dr. N.B. Biswas and Mr. Dipankar. We are equally thankful to Mr. Supratim Choudhury and SCube, Silchar, for typing assistance. We also thank Mr. Shankar Sen and Mr. Debashis Chowdhury for programming and electronic assistance.

The views expressed in the papers are those of individual authors and the editors are not responsible for these. However, for any errors despite our sincere efforts, the responsibility lies only on us.

Contents

III. Inusrgency, Human Rights: Towards A Counter Discourse

Introduction

Human Rights (HR) discourse in contemporary times has become an effective institutional tool for the State to impose authoritarian self-serving agenda on the people. The rhetoric of HR expresses a moral concern based on the assumption that human beings possess certain individual rights which should be guarded against the State or groups that violate them. Paradoxically the institutional network of the State, grounds the justification of State intervention on the lives of individuals setting matters right on this moral concern. In a sense, the State tends to own the moral concern of a milieu. As it mobilises popular consent in support of such intervention and calls it a 'humanitarian concern', it becomes rather difficult to make an acceptable critique of this intervention.[1] A true human rights culture is thus juxtaposed to the politics of HR, manouvered by the State. Any interrogation of the basic premise of HR must be read today with reference to this bifurcation. Surprisingly, the issue of HR is being discussed at the level of an utopian ideal rather than being considered in relation to power. The international crusade for HR has been institutionalised through a variety of international organisations and NGOs. A clear manifestation of this approach can be found in most UN publications. A case in point is the UN Secretary General D. Boutros Ghali's report in 1992, which represents a strategic affirmation for the diplomacy of HR, turning the UN into a global police force. Not only the UN but even organisations focussing on hard economic issues like the World Bank claim to be 'humane' and 'people centered' and thus, adopt the new humanitarian rhetoric of human rights discourse. At the level of rhetoric, it is difficult to object to an international perspective, which claims to be people centered and ethical. However, HR is not only an intellectual project or an exercise in ethics. The UN, in practice, has hardly raised its voice against military interventions, organised violence and coersion. Since its inception in the 1940s, the UN has initiated 34 peace-keeping operations which are rarely criticised. Today, HR advocates uphold their argument as an expression of self evident universal rights that no one can question. Article 55 of the United Nations Declaration on Human Rights (1948) states that the UN shall "promote universal respect for and observance of human rights and fundamental freedoms for all". Article 56 states .... "all members pledge themselves to take joint and separate action in co-operation with the organisation for the achievement of the purpose set forward in Article 55". The debates surrounding the Declaration of Human Rights indicate that there has been little consensus about what constitutes a human right. The HR concept, therefore, became a trump card through which "diplomatic priorities of the most powerful nations have turned into a universal objective for others, turning aside the voice of weaker nations."[2]

The originary violation of HR takes place when an institutional authority like the UN or the State becomes the custodian of individual or collective rights. The most prominent feature of modern Nation-State is its role as the 'hegemonic actor in the public realm'. From matters of art and literature to the field of sports, virtually every sphere of life is under the jurisdiction of the State.[3] The emergence of the post-colonial Indian state gave birth to an elite leadership which tried to function with an imported concept of statecraft and legitimised the concept, invoking India's past culture. One of the expectations involved in this strategy was that modernity would diminish the diversities of the Indian nation. The other expectation of the ruling elite was that principles of the statecraft would adjust to the dominant State ideology. The strategy of nation building sought to integrate the minority cultures with the dominant ones instead of a recognition of specifics of cultures. Obviously, the Indian State became the central arbitrator in setling ethnic or religious conflicts. Etienne Balbir uses the term 'fictive ethnicity' to denote the community instituted by the nation-state to legitimise its 'presence'.[4] 'Fictive ethnicity' is not patriotism but an invocation of the past 'historic mission' against which the present is measured and which justifies the strategies employed by the State to control the masses. It attributes only one identity to an individual and interpellates the individual in the name of the collective, where human essence is eroded. Collectivity becomes a great threat to civil rights when the nation defines collective individuals standardising them by negative differences. A nation has its own culture industry through which it labels individuals, categorises people and creates images of the nation and the human being. Plurality is the essence of a human being and so human essence is lost when the nation produces certain stereotypes of individuals and communities.

Conceptualising HR requires understanding of what rights one possesses by virtue of being 'human'. Having 'rights' does not necessarily mean that one is a 'human being'. Rather one is a human being with human rights when one has rights simply because one is a human being irrespective of varying social circumstances.[5] Rights are there to strengthen human or collective identity and violations of these rights take place when nation disfigures certain identities, erasing specific differences and replacing them with artificial differences. Arbitrary nature of creating differences and legitimising them through the culture industry is one of the highest violations of HR in any civil society. The idea of HR becomes a misnomer and an idealistic illusion in a society where the means of production of economy and culture rest with a few. Concepts like law, justice, morality, democracy, freedom and HR cannot be regarded as fixed historical categories, for, as the conditions of life and material forces change, the content of notions and ideas may also change. Differences among individuals and groups also change under historical and cultural circumstances. Besides, all differences are not necessarily conflictual in nature and so erasing differences on a flat scale or imposing similarities would negate the 'dialectics of differences'. Rights are assigned by the State, institutioanlised and then legitimised by it through its agencies. The State uses violence to implement those rights or guard the violation of these rights. In either case, power and violence in covert or overt form become the weapon of the State. Imaginary tales of 'epistemic violence' and its sources are constructed by the State to suit its ideology. Structural violence is involved in the very construction of national imagery, through writing of partial histories and claiming totality. This violation is also evident in the imposition of 'sex' on gender, gender being a cultural construct of the patriarchal ideology of the State. Woman as sex subject is the "crucial 'site' upon which battles are waged between tradition and modernity, nationalism and colonialism."[6] Besides, the imposition of national or State languages, the forced inscription of dominant national symbols and uniform also constitute structural and epistemic violation of HR.

Domination in civil societies arrange identities against each other and resist transcendence and intercultural mixing, which transgress the rigidly defined limits of an identity. Once such an arrangement becomes a social reality, the contest among various identities get shifted from 'contest of definite markers' to contest over issues of encroachment and transgression of the narrow limits of identities. Thus, the nature of the conflict among various identities depend on how the immediately contestable 'other' behaves and acts. The colonial State produced a public space in which the defined limits of various identities were ruffled against one another in the sites of production, politics and administration. This is how modernity reinforced the dominant-dominated relationship in cultural terms, where one identity saw the 'other' as a threat to its existence. The Indian nationalist discourse operating through such a contest ridden public space mediated the intercultural relationship between communities without addressing their specific culture claims. And so, instead of a nation emerging from the cultural grass-roots, a colonial mosaic of dominance and Statecraft was superimposed. The nationalist ideology of post-colonial India operated through the interest of the social and cultural dominant groups and so invited resistance from non-dominant ones. The Indian State thrives on the retention of the dominance of particular social identities and uses coercion to establish its authority through these identities. The State assumes a hegemonic presence through the use of force and manipulates the process of identity construction, projecting some identities as more dominant than the others.

Counter-hegemonic struggle like Insurgency, instead of striking at the root of Statist ideology, is mostly directed against the socially rooted dominance. The monological agenda of Insurgency is that of the subversion of nationalism and the reforming of smaller identities within the dominant social identity recognised by the State. Insurgency in the North East India claims to represent the non-dominant and subaltern identities. Here, the 'nation' as a metaphor of the dominant social identity is contested in the struggle of the insurgent groups for cultural and political autonomy. 'Internal decolonization'[7], has produced a contradictory situation of the duality of the 'civic citizen' and the 'native citizen' and also an alternative layer of exclusive membership of citizens as subjects of native communities. In North East India, the maintenance of socially rooted dominance in the political space has been exhibited in the effort to create separate provinces for various tribes and communities—such as Nagaland for Nagas, Meghalaya for Khasis, Jaintias and Garos, Mizoram for Mizos. Counter-hegemonic struggle also bases its social action on violence. Thus, violence becomes a weapon of both the hegemonic and counter-hegemonic players. Besides, insurgents may not always be counter-hegemonic players, because they do not attack the Statist architecture of violence. Insurgency does not interrogate the institutional build up of the State in which social highways are created and the rituals of the constitutional passages are established. Insurgency does not address itself to the fundamental question of class which is the starting point of analysis of a class-divided society.[8] The essence of Insurgency is such that certain expectations are aroused without a sense of accountability. However, the State as a social actor of violence uses armed force to suppress anything that comes on its way. It seeks to acquire legitimacy from within by activating more of military violence. Insurgency, on the other hand, strives to get legitimacy from without by making an ideological critique of the State and, ironically, pursuing the same agenda of power. In the North East the State is suffering a crisis of legitimacy, but it is functioning forcefully representing antagonistic interests. Insurgency, contrary to its claims, does not identify itself with subaltern class interests and operates in a mode that reinforces the legitimacy of State apparatus.

II

The concept of HR has been in existence since many centuries either as 'natural law', 'natural rights' or 'positive rights' though the internationalisation of the concept started only half a century back with the adoption of the Universal Declaration of Human Rights by the UN (1946). Since then the UN has attempted to define and formulate the concept through various convenants and instruments. The Indian Constitution guarantees its citizens fundamental rights such as right to life, liberty, equality, freedom and protection against inhuman treatment and cruelty. These are in essence, what the HR seeks to achieve for the people. In India, HR is defined under the Protection of Human Rights Act, 1993 as follows (S.N. Bhargava):

> Human Rights means the rights relating to life, liberty, equality and dignity of the individual guaranteed by the Constitution or embodied in the International Covenant and enforceable by courts in India.

The practice of HR underlines problem of demarcating the area of freedom and authority. It is not unoften that the need to maintain the territorial integrity and sovereignty of a country clashes with the autonomy aspirations of groups within the country. Bhargava succinctly points out: 'it is an irony of human existence that one man's spirit of independence is the other man's crime of terrorism or insurgency.'

India is known internationally to champion the rights of States fighting colonialism and racist regime but at the same time, it is one such country which has faced the autonomy and liberation movements.

These movements, be it in Assam, Nagaland, Mizoram or Manipur, rationalize their demand on the basis of cultural or minority rights and historical antecedents. Hence, demand for the exercise of right of national self-determination is raised time and again. The Government has sought to resolve the problem by advocating counter insurgency. This policy has resulted in atrocities committed by the military and para-military forces on the insurgents and civilians alike. Thus, a country which claims to have won political independence on the principle of non-violence has opted for violent means to maintain its territorial integrity and sovereignty.

Any discussion on the counter-insurgency policy remains incomplete without a reference to the Armed Forces Special Powers Act, 1958. Bhargava, Dhamala and Nag discuss the various provisions under the Act and show how the application of those powers put a small premium on the ethics of HR. Various operations such as Singjmei and Blue Bird to flush out the so called insurgents, have brought untold misery, torture and extra-judicial execution. To bring succour to the people in the face of such atrocities HR organisations like CLAHRO and NPMHR have been formed. These organisations have been working consistently towards the spread of HR awareness among the people as also to bring relief to the victims by seeking administrative and judicial remedy (Dhamala). Narrating the history of these atrocities, Nag shows how these are translated into their folk tales and folk songs.

To be fair to the Army, it must be remembered that the State policy has been to call the Army when the situation goes out of control and the administration fails to contain the situation. They are not called at the preventive stage. According to T. Mukherjee 'special laws are essential both for operating as also to protect individuals against long-drawn legal battles for action taken in good faith to restore normalcy.'

There are cases of violence committed by the Insurgents and the Army. The obvious suffers in the process are the people whose rights are subjected to violations. To protect the people from the abuse of their rights it is essential to spread the HR knowledge not only among the army personnel but also among the people. To strengthen the HR movement N.B. Biswas suggests that HR education should constitute one of the essential components of school curriculum. The curriculum as developed by him puts special emphasis on value education which would help in the character formation of the young people and also make them aware of the concept and practices of HR.

It is admitted that since the Independence, the NE India is embroiled in conflict-like situations. The Naga uprising, the struggle carried by the MNF for an independent Mizoram was followed by a process of ethnic conflict such as in Meghalaya, Assam, Manipur etc. The general attitude is to externalise the problem by blaming either the non-tribals or the Centre. This obviously refers to the role of the State in the development process of any region. Since the inception of the planned programmes, the NE region has been exposed to various development experiments. These programmes are developed without taking into consideration the socio-cultural context. As a result of the implementation of ill-conceived planned programmes and the sudden exposure of the society to outside influences certain disfunctionalities began to appear. (C.K. Biswas; Tanmoy Bhattacharjee).

This has created social cleavages and differences in the otherwise classless tribal society. The rapid monetisation of the economy led to exploitation of the people. In order to ensure popular participation in the political process as also to develop the region as per the local needs, the Autonomous District Councils have been established. But Tanmoy Bhattacharjee, citing the case of Haflong Autonomous District Council, points out the failure of these institutions to integrate the traditional institutions. These institutions have emphasised over bureaucratisation and have ignored the youths and their aspirations. These disgruntled youths have been recruited and used by different insurgent outfits. Here, the need is not only to empower the people but also to take into account the socio-cultural context.

These planned programmes have not only ignored the socio-cultural context but also the ecological aspect which has received scant attention from the planners. The objective of sustainable development has failed to evolve. Consequently, incursions into the fragile ecology of the region led to the rapid depletion of resources resulting in stiff resource-competition among the various groups. Naturally, the non-tribals, immigrants and the so-called foreigners had to face expulsion or the threat of expulsion. This can be exemplified by referring to instances of ethnic conflicts in the region (Abhik Gupta). Under the prevailing situation, on the one hand, the legitimacy of the State stands questioned and the developmental programmes fail to achieve the stated goals, on the other.

The discussion on HR brings into focus the issues of minority rights, the emergence of various ethnic groups through constant redefinition of ethnic boundaries and above all the justification for the existence of State as the guarantor of human rights and freedom.

In a multi-ethnic society the definition of minority is beset with problems since the status of majority-minority is not constant in the Indian context. In the NE India the (national) minority (otherwise regional majority) has been provided with constitutional safegaurds and privileges but to what extent has this has protected and furthered the cause of minority in the region, *i.e.* the non-tribals of the region, is an open question. The dichotomy in the interpretation of the majority-minority status has led to the violations of the HR of the regional minorities but these have failed to receive national attention. This reflects the gap between the principles and practices of HR as also between universalism and particularism. (Rajesh Dev).

Human Rights has become one of the agencies of the State to propagate its ideology and justify the existence of the machineries of violence and coersion. The hegemonic presence of the State has been appropriated by Insurgent uprising as evident in the North-Eastern context. However, Insurgency in its failure to make a critique of the logic of the capital has fallen into the drama of violence and HR violation like the State. B. S. Butola, Prasenjit Biswas and Sukalpa Bhattacharjee make a critique of the formation of the Indian Nation-State and discuss how structual violence is involved in the very history and ideology of the State apparatus. Prasenjit Biswas examines the 'new subaltern' emergence of the identities of NE India and the birth of 'nations from below'. Sukalpa Bhattachargee's paper examines the cultural construction of gender in an ethnic community, where the (wo)man as a bracketed entity experiences an exclusion both from the public space of a Nation or Human Rights and from the discourses of ethnic resistance manifest in Insurgency. And yet she is the common site/sight of both the warring sides for the inscription of violence. Sukalpa Bhattacharjee analyses how from such a peripheral position, the ethnic woman reclaims her cultural rights as HR and reconstructs her (self) as an ethno-sexual subject. B. S. Butola states that HR is a misnomer in a Capitalist State and will remain so till the policy of 'internal colonization persists.' Prasenjit Biswas offers a perspective of ethnic and communnitarian resistance, by way of the ethno-cultural construction of the' nations from below', which is interrogating the State hegemony that operates through this 'internal decolonization' of the State. The parameter of HR violation is very fuzzy and the common people are the ultimate victims, whether the State uses force to curb Insurgency or the Insurgents take to armed struggle to destabilise the power of the State.

Under such circumstances the emphasis of the State on fraternity, friendship, peace and harmony is philosophically vacuous becasue it does not contain the spirit of genuine multiculturalism. In "Right' Consciousness and the 'Other': A Parapolitical Approach", Goutam Biswas maintains that violation of HR takes place when 'right consciousness' is monopolised by a dominant group to marginalise the smaller groups. The degradation of the dignity, freedom and liberty of the people as a result of this dominant versus marginal contest, in the hands of State authoirty and the Insurgents alike, can be mitigated only if the 'other' in the community is recognised and accepted. He visualises the solution of the problem in the social translation of the notion of 'Swaraj' as developed by Gandhiji. The politics of tension can be resolved by creating a space for dialogue among diverse ethnic and cultural groups for the restoration of HR.

NOTES AND REFERENCES

1. Kofi Buenor Hadjor, "Whose Human Rights?", *Journal of Asian and African Studies*, Vol, XXXIII, No. 4, November 1998.
2. *Ibid.* Hadjor makes an objective analysis and critique of the institutionalisation of Human Rights at the international level.
3. Ashis Nandy, "The Political Culture of the Indian State": *Daedalus* 118(4): 1-26, 1989, discusses how democracy itself is the victim of the new political culture of the Nation State.
4. Etienne Balibar, "The Nation Form: History and Ideology" trans. Immanuel Wallerstein (Part-I) and Chris Turner (Part-II) in *Race, Nation, Class*. London, Verso, 1990.
5. Jerome J. Shestak, former US ambassador to the UN Commission on Human Rights, asks the question 'What is meant by Human Rights? in "The Philosophic Foundation of Human Rights," *Human Rights Quarterly*, 20, 1998, 201-234.
6. Ania Loomba and Suvir Kaul elaborate this point of tension between 'sex' and gender in 'Location, Culture, Post-coloniality,' *Oxford Literary Review*: Special issue on India Vol. 16.1/2, 1994.
7. The concept of 'internal decolonization' has been discussed also by Jan Nederveen Pieterse and Bhikhu Parekh in "Shifting imaginary : decolonization, internal decolonization, post-coloniality" in Jan Nederveen Pieterse and Bhikhu Parekh ed. *The Decolonization of Imagination: Culture, Knowledge and Power*. OUP, Delhi, 1997.
8. Karl Marx: *The Economic and Philosophic Manuscripts* of 1844 (Martin Milligan trans., Dirk J. Struik ed, 1969) cited in *Ibid.*

I ~ Conceptualising Human Rights

1

Human Rights and Low Intensity: Conflicts in India

S. N. Bhargava

Concept and Background

The concept of Human Rights is based on the theory that a man is born free. Soon after his birth he gets inalienable right to live with dignity which should not be trampled down by outside agencies. Human Rights can be generally defined as those rights which are inherent in our nature and without which we cannot live as human beings. The very word Human Rights denotes that it is fundamental and belongs to every human being. Human Rights is the foundation of human existence and co-existence. It is universal, indivisible and inter-dependent.

Human Rights is the expression of those traditions of tolerance embodied in all religions and cultures that are the basis of peace and progress. It is foreign to no culture but native to all nations. In all cultures tolerance and mercy have always been ideals of government rule and human behaviour.

What is most precious to any man is his life. Next to that is his personal liberty. That is why life and liberty are two basic components of human rights. The moment a person comes in the womb he gets his Human Rights. A pregnant mother should have good nourishment so that she maintains good health for proper development of the foetus. As soon as one is born, he is entitled to good health, good nourishment, pure air to breath, unadulterated food to eat, pure water to drink, place to live, clothes to cover his body and facilities for education and employment and to both physical and mental development.

The concept of Human Rights is as old as Declaration of

Independence when in the year 1776 nearly 220 years ago, the second Continental Congress attended by delegates from English Colonies in North America adopted the 'Declaration of Independence'. Then came the French Revolution in 1789 which symbolised the end of Autocracy in France. The National Assembly of France adopted 'Declaration of Rights of Man and Citizen' which was truly international in its appeal and inspired revolutionary and democratic movements in almost every country of Europe and in Central and South America and later, in Asia and Africa. Then came the revolution in Russia in 1917. All Russian Congress of Soviets adopted the 'Declaration of the Rights of the Working and Exploited People'.

Concept of Human Rights started developing gradually throughout the world. After the Second World War was over, the United Nations Charter was adopted in 1945 which reflected the aspirations of the people who had been engaged in the war against fascist barbarism and affirmed faith in 'Fundamental Human Rights' and in the dignity and worth of human beings. The General Assembly of the United Nations adopted and proclaimed the 'Universal Declaration of Human Rights' on 10th December 1948, which is being observed as a World Human Rights Day every year.

Conventions on Human Rights

The International Convention on elimination of all forms of racial discrimination was adopted by the General Assembly of the United Nations on 21st December, 1965. The Universal Declaration of Human Rights provided the basis for the formulation by the United Nations' covenants and conventions, declarations and recommendations on specific aspects. Three documents—The Universal Declaration of Human Rights, the International Covenant on Civil and Political Rights and the International Covenant on Economic, Social and Cultural Rights alongwith two protocols—Optional Protocols to the International Covenant on Civil and Political Rights, and the Second Optional Protocol to the International Covenant on Civil and Political Rights, constitute the International Bill of Human Rights which was adopted by the General Assembly of the United Nations on 16th December, 1966 and came into force on 3rd January 1976. Convention against torture and other cruel, inhuman or degrading treatment or punishment was adopted by the General Assembly of the United Nations on 10th December 1984 and came into force on 26th June, 1987.

The general framework of Human Rights which was affirmed in international declarations and covenants was mainly concerned with rights of individuals. A landmark development in the formulation and recognition of new Human Rights is the Declaration on the Right to Development which was adopted by the General Assembly of the United Nations on 4th December, 1986. This Declaration is particularly significant far the developing countries, even though the necessary means for enforcing it are still lacking. Convention on the Rights of the Child was adopted by the General Assembly of the United Nations on 20th November, 1989 and came into force on 2nd September 1990. Convention on the elimination of all forms of discrimination against women was adopted by the General Assembly of the United Nations on 18th December, 1979 and came into force on 3rd September 1981. But the scenario has not changed and violence against women continues. Therefore, the United Nations General Assembly in December 1993 passed by consensus a declaration on the elimination of violence against women.

A World Conference on Human Rights was held at Vienna, Austria in 1993 which was attended by about 7,000 participants representing 171 countries. In the Conference progress made in the field of Human Rights since the adoption of Universal Declaration of Human Rights in 1948, was assessed, reviewed and future programme of action was charted.

Human Rights in India

So far India is concerned Human Rights has been defined under the Protection of Human Rights Act, 1993 in the following words:

> "Human Rights" means the right relating to life, liberty, equality and dignity of the individual guaranteed by the Constitution or embodied in the International Covenant and enforceable by Courts in India.

In India we have always believed in the dignity of human beings and always protected the human rights. Our culture and heritage and belief is that God exists in every human being. If you want to serve God you should serve human being. We have always believed in *vasudev kutumbakam* and also *sarve bhavantu sukhenah sarve santo niramayah.* We always pray *loka samasta sukhino bhabantu.* We consider the whole world as one family and pray—let everyone be happy and prosperous.

If India could win freedom by non-violence why cannot we build India by non-violence? After the Independence gradually terrorism and insurgency have developed particularly in Jammu and Kashmir, Punjab and the North East because of communal animosity, mistrust, lack of employment opportunities and economic compulsion. Democracy requires respect for life and rule of law. Democracy cannot be sustained if terrorism and insurgency continue, nor can it accommodate those who seek power through terror and cold blooded murder of innocent civilians.

The present society has brought upon mankind a great challenge due to the violation of Human Rights in the hands of the terrorists, because terrorism retards the process for social development. It contravenes the generally accepted norms of social order—right to life, right of existence and survival and equality of all human beings and, above all, it is retrogressive.

It is an irony of human existence that one man's spirit of independence is the other man's crime of terrorism or insurgency. Therefore, there is a need of human rights protagonists to draw a line between the two extreme ends in order to arrive at acceptable levels of resistance.

Background of the "The Armed Forces Special Powers Act 1958"

Law and order has to be maintained primarily by civil police. The State Government is responsible for the same through its Director General of Police and the whole paraphernalia under him. But during the last two decades army has been deployed to maintain internal law and order situation in several States of the North Eastern region and Jammu & Kashmir. Central Government thought it proper to deploy Armed Forces to help the civil administration in maintaining law and order situation and the Parliament considered it proper to invest certain special powers upon the members of the Armed Forces in disturbed areas and enacted the law "The Armed Forces (Special Powers) Act 1958" which repealed the earlier ordinance on that subject.

In the Parliament debates of the Lok Sabha in 1958, Pandit G.B. Pant, the then Minister of Home Affairs, opined "Armed Forces Special Powers Bill is a very simple measure to enable certain special powers to be conferred upon members of the armed forces in disturbed areas in the State of (the then) Assam and the Union Territory of Manipur. It only seeks to protect the steps that the armed forces might have to take in the disturbed areas. It is not possible over such a vast area to depute civil magistrates to accompany the armed forces wherever there may be trouble, because it happens unexpectedly. They might intrude into any village and action has to be taken immediately".

Pandit Pant further observed: "It does not create any new offences. It only provides for the protection of the army when it has to deal with hostile Nagas". Further, "No power is transferred from the executive authority. The magistrates are there. The police is there. All other activities which are usually in the hands of the civil administration will, even hereafter be in their hands". While replying to the debate Panditji pointed out: "the Armed Forces are under the Central Government. The Central Government can use them in any way it likes. Under the law, the civil authority even in States can seek the assistance of the Armed Forces whenever they are faced with disturbed conditions".

During the debate, Shri Mahanty referred the Bill as a "unique legislation, the kind of which has never been contemplated. Regulation is not legislation; it is an administrative and executive fiat. What I am trying to submit is that this is a martial law. This is martial law as defined in Article 34 of the Constitution."

Salient Features of the Act

Section 3 of the said Act empowers States to declare areas to be disturbed areas, if the whole or any part of the State is in such disturbed or in dangerous condition that the use of Armed Force in aid of civil administration is necessary. Section 4 confers on any commissioned officer, warrant officer, non-commissioned officer or any other person of equivalent rank in the Armed Forces in disturbed areas, the powers enumerated in clauses (a) to (d). Clause (a) empowers officers of Armed Forces in certain contingencies contemplated therein to use force. Clause(b) authorises them in certain contingencies to destroy any arms dump or fortified position or shelter or structures. Clause (c) empowers such members of Armed forces in a disturbed area to arrest without warrant any person who has committed a cognisable offence or against whom a reasonable suspicion exists that he has committed or is about to commit a cognisable offence and to use such force as may be necessary to effect the arrest. Clause (d) empowers the officers to enter and search without warrant any premises to make any such arrests as aforesaid or to recover any person believed to be wrongfully restrained or confined or any property reasonably suspected to be stolen property or any arms, ammunition or explosive substances believed to be unlawfully kept in such premise, and for that purpose to use force as may be necessary. Section 5 of the Act requires that any person so arrested and taken into custody shall be handed over to the officer-in-charge of the nearest police station with the least possible delay, together with a report of the circumstances occasioning the arrest.

Section 6 provides that no prosecution, suit or other legal proceeding shall be instituted, except with the previous sanction of the Central Government, against any person in respect of anything done or purported to be done in exercise of the powers conferred by this Act. The constitutionality of this Act was challenged in several writ petitions before the Gauhati High Court which were transferred to the Delhi High Court by the Supreme Court. The Delhi High Court upheld the constitutionality of this Act. It was also held that the Army authority acting under the provisions of these Acts can arrest a person without any invitation on the part of and without reference to the police authority of the State in disturbed areas.

In *Bacha Bora vs. State of Assam* (1991)2 GLR: 119 case, a division bench held that the words 'least possible delay' mean 'within the shortest possible time' though no arbitrary time limit can be set down as it may not be possible in many cases to affirmatively say or precisely quantify the period of time by reference to hours, dates or months, and whenever the question arises for decision for computing the period of time, the Court has to have regard to the particular circumstances of the case; for example, physical impossibility or otherwise to hand over the arrested person to the nearest police station and to report how and under what circumstances the arrest was effected.

Clause(c) of Section 4 of the Act contemplates two contingencies: *viz.* (a) where a person has committed a cognisable offence, undoubtedly there will be some materials on the basis of which a conclusion to that effect is arrived at and (b) existence of reasonable suspicion either that a person has committed a cognisable offence or that he is about to commit a cognisable offence. The legislature used the words 'reasonable suspicion exists' and not words like 'reason to believe' or 'satisfaction' which are words importing stronger conviction. The word 'reasonable' and 'suspicion' are easily comprehensible. But it is difficult to define them particularly in a context where they are used in juxtaposition to each other. The word 'suspicion' is indicative of a cognisable offence which has either been committed or is about to be committed. But suspicion should not be baseless or based upon sheer intuition. It is to be based upon some relevant materials though such materials may not be tantamount to legal evidence or proof. It is these relevant materials which may render a suspicion 'reasonable'. If the circumstances as revealed in the Army authorities' report or the subsequent questioning by police lead to the inference that the person is involved in the commission of a cognisable offence, it is the duty of the police to register a case and deal with the arrested person in accordance with the procedure prescribed in the Criminal Procedure Code. If they are of the opinion that he is about to commit a cognisable offence it is open to them to deal with him under the preventive provisions of the Code of Criminal Procedure or any other law for the time being in force.

Armed Forces have been conferred certain extraordinary powers under the Act with a view to aid the civil authority. Such powers have been conferred on the assumption that the ground situation in a disturbed area is so bad and chaotic and the law and order situation so poor that civil authority cannot always be trusted to arrest person who have committed cognisable offences or are about to commit cognisable offences. The legislature thought it fit that Armed Forces under those circumstances must act in aid of the civil authority. This has been done for the well-being of the people. At the same time legislature has mandated that those arrested should be handed over to the civil authority with the least possible delay. This is how the legislature seeks to maintain balance between the conflicting claims of public interest and individual liberty. The existing law protects people who are taken into custody by civil police.

Armed Forces and the Supreme Court

This Act was challenged in the High Court and later on it came up before the Supreme Court of India along with other connected matters and the same was disposed of by order dated 27th November 1997. A five Judges Bench upheld the instructions issued by the Central Government giving a list of Do's and Don'ts while acting under Armed Forces (Special Powers) Act 1958 which would provide effective checks against any misuse or abuse of the powers conferred. The Supreme Court of India opined that these instructions should be treated as binding instructions that are required to be followed by the members of the Armed Forces while exercising powers under the Central Act. Any violation of instructions and the person/persons found guilty of such violation should be suitably punished under the Army Act of 1950. The Supreme Court also suggested that certain observations made by the Supreme Court while deciding such cases should be incorporated in the instructions contained in the list of Do's and Don'ts and the instructions should be suitably amended to bring them in conformity with the guidelines contained in the decision of the Supreme Court in this regard. It further observed that a complaint against misuse or abuse of the powers conferred under the Act should be thoroughly enquired into and if it is found that there is substance in the allegation, the victim should be suitably compensated by the State and the requisite sanction under Section 6 of the Central Act should be granted for institution of prosecution and/or a civil suit or the proceeding against the person/ persons responsible for such violation.

Armed Forced and Our Nation

Armed Forces have ensured national stability, promoted national integrity and provided national defence. They have materially contributed to the functioning of democracy in India. It must maintain highest standard of discipline, professionalism, leadership, gallantry and devotion. Overuse of armed forces in internal security duties can be counter productive. The Army is expected to defend the frontiers or the boundaries of the country and to fight against the enemies. Unfortunately, Army is now being engaged in aid of civil administration to fight terrorism and armed insurgency. Military is primarily trained to deal with the enemies only and naturally, is not expected to deal with its own brethren. But once the Army is called to help the civil administration it should be left entirely to the Army to control the situation without any interference from the civil administration or politicians. If the army is not permitted or allowed to act according to its own plans, the whole purpose would be lost. The Indian Army has earned its name in the whole world and has always been conscious of Human Rights. Even in ancient times this country had the tradition of maintaining Human Rights at the time of active war in Mahabharata at Kurukshetra.

The protection of Human Rights in areas afflicted by terrorism or armed insurgency poses special problems. Use of force is essential to curb terrorism and insurgency. But Human Rights also should be kept in mind on such occasions. Terrorism is a negation and violation of norms of human behaviour recognised by all civilised people of the world. It contravenes the generally accepted norms of social order, right to life, right of existence and survival and equality of all human beings and, above all, it is retrogressive.

The security forces are generally called upon to assist the civil administration in areas afflicted with terrorism or insurgency, the forces must act in close co-ordination with the civil administration. They must perform their duty to the nation to fight and triumph over terrorism.

They must observe international standards of Human Rights and discharge their duty with full respect for the laws of the land and the rights of all the people. The rights of the victims of terrorism and armed militancy should not be neglected but they should be assisted by all appropriate means.

Armed forces are essentially trained and equipped for anti-militant operation or war activities against enemies. Army Chief Shanker Roy Choudhury has recently said that the Indian Army is the number one fighting force in the world and will maintain its position. Yet, Indian Army needs to be modernised and it is being done with the available resources.

Conclusion with Suggestions

There has been increasing thought given both at the national and the international level to ways in which terrorism can be countered and eliminated without vitiating human rights principles.

International conventions and treaties pertaining to Human Rights do not recognise terrorist violence as legitimate action arising out of any ideological commitments. Any such precept cannot be given precedence over Human Rights and no such action can validate terrorism anywhere in the world, for, there can be no freedom which impinges upon freedoms, no equality which upholds inequality and there can be no life which pretends death. It has been particularly helpful that, since the 1993 Vienna Conference, greater intellectual clarity has emerged on this vexed issue and that this finds expression, most notably, in recent proceedings and resolutions of the United Nations Commission on Human Rights (UNCHR) and the General Assembly. They adopted two resolutions: (1) relating to 'Measures to Eliminate International Terrorism', and (2) 'Human Rights and Terrorism'. The resolution of the UNCHR provides *inter-alia* 'criminal acts intended or calculated to provoke a state of terror in the general public, a group of persons or particular persons for political purposes are in any circumstances unjustifiable whatever the considerations of a political, philosophical, ideological, racial, religious or any other nature that may be invoked to justify them'. The General Assembly resolution after reiterating its 'unequivocal condemnation of the acts, methods and practices of terrorism as activities aimed at the destruction of Human Rights, fundamental freedoms and democracy called upon States "to take all necessary and effective measures in accordance with international standards of Human Rights to prevent, combat and eliminate all acts of terrorism whenever and wherever committed".

To conclude, I would like to suggest that Human Rights education should be imparted to jawans. It is but essential to give an Indian orientation to the thinking of the Army. These must be elucidated with due emphasis in the context of cultural, social and religious background of security forces personnel. They must be given an effective re-orientation before they are deployed in new areas and should also be constantly and repeatedly reminded of basic Human Rights.

The armed forces should be sensitised regarding the issue of Human Rights. They should set up watch-dogs right from headquarters down to division level. Any complaint received should be promptly investigated and acted upon. This concept of Human Rights should not only remain confined to the officers but should trickle down to jawans and soldiers as well.

Seminars and symposia, debates or essay writing competitions on Human Rights for army personnel at different levels should be held quite often to sensitise them. Circulars containing detailed instructions should be issued and circulated from time to time to make army personnel aware of the Human Rights.

Army should operate in close co-operation with the civil administration. Use of excessive force should be avoided. Officers and soldiers should be given education and training on Human Rights in all the courses conducted by the Army so that awareness is created.

Former Prime Minister I.K. Gujral during his visit to the North East India had observed: "Army which operates in difficult terrains and remote place is known for its dedication, valour, discipline and loyalty to the nation. We are proud of the Army. They have brought laurels to the country with peace keeping operations in different parts of the world including Somalia, Angola, etc." He called upon the Army to carry out their job with professionalism and human approach.

Due to the insurgency problem in the North East, the Army has been deployed in the region for more than four decades, but as the problems are essentially political in character, the approach to resolving such problem must also be political.

2

Human Rights

Safeguards and Violations

Ranju R. Dhamala

The concern for rights of humans has been in evidence throughout the range of recorded history. Early philosophers addressed themselves to the issues of 'natural law', 'natural rights' or 'positive rights'. The Renaissance and the Age of Enlightenment furthered the cause of the rights of humans to remain free and equal. The signing of Magna Carta in 1215 was a significant step towards codifying these rights; the Bill of Rights, 1689 consolidated the important rights and liberty of the people; the U.S. Bill of Rights became a part of the American Constitution in December 1791 and these rights therefrom received a constitutional status. The development in the field of Human Rights continued throughout the 19th and the 20th centuries. Different exigencies such as fight against slavery, humanitarian concern for the prisoners of war and the occurrence of the two world wars led to this development.

In the 20th century, concern for international peace and harmony consequent upon the ravages of two world wars led to evolution of the concept of Human Rights from its earlier formulations to its contemporary explications. The concept of Human Rights today evinces two clearly irreconcilable aspects, *viz.,* rhetorics/propagation and violation. These two aspects manifest a gap between the principles centering round human rights and their practice. While the moral and philosophical validity of the concept is unquestionable and reverence for human life and goals of peace, freedom and equality motivated many countries to codify the rights of humans and guarantee such rights to people, cases of violations of human rights are also ample. These violations are rooted not only in the lack of political morality but also in the inefficiency of the State to fulfill its responsibilities towards its citizens. In practice however, attempt has always been to avoid a blantant violation of human rights by striking a balance between principles and practices within the statist framework. Hence, a continuous review and reinterpretation of the concept can be traced over the last fifty years.

In what follows, I propose to examine the human rights against this background. With an outline of the provisions of the HR under various UN Convenants and other Instruments I shall examine the principles and practices of the HR in India particularly in the context of North-East India.

II

The United Nations has described human rights as inherent in our nature and as those without which we cannot live as human beings. The concept includes a whole range of rights which are essential not only for individual's freedom but also for the overall development of human personality. With this objective, the Universal Declaration of Human Rights was adopted in 1948 and the International Covenant on Economic, Sócial and Cultural Rights and International Covenant on Civil and Political Rights were adopted by the General Assembly in 1966 which came into force in 1976.

The Declaration consists of a preamble and 30 Articles. It recognises the inherent dignity and equal inalienable rights of all members of the human family as the foundation of freedom, justice and peace in the world. It also recognises the right to life, liberty and security of persons and equality before law.

The International Covenant on Economic Social and Cultural Rights has a preamble and 31 Articles divided into five parts. It contains a long list of economic, social and cultural rights. Part I (Article 1) speaks of the right of self determination of people. Part II (Articles 2-5) enjoins upon the signatory states to take steps 'individually and through international assistance and cooperation, especially economic and technical, to the maximum of its available resources' for the realisation of rights recognised in the present Covenant 'by all appropriate means, including particularly the adoption of legislative measures'. These states may subject the rights mentioned in the Covenant only 'to such limitations as are determined by law' and required for 'promoting the general welfare in a democratic society', but no State can derogate from any fundamental human rights 'on the pretext that the present Covenant does not recognize them to a lesser extent'. Part III (Articles 6-15) includes a long list of the social, economic and cultural rights, such as right to work, right of everyone to the enjoyment of just and favourable conditions of work, right to form trade union, right to social security including social insurance, right of everyone to an adequate standard of living, right to education, right to take part in cultural life to enjoy benefits of scientific progress and its application. The Covenant does not merely list these rights but also describes and defines them in considerable detail and states the steps that should be taken for their full realisation by the signatory parties. Although all the above rights are considered essential for the economic, social and cultural well being of the States, Article 2(3) mentions that the developing countries with due regard to human rights and their national economy, may determine the extent to which they would guarantee the economic rights recognized in the present Covenant to non-nationals. Part IV (Articles 16-25) includes the measures necessary for the proper implementation of the Covenant. According to Article 16 (1,2,a,b), the signatory states would submit reports on the measures adopted and progress made in achieving the observance of the rights to the Secretary General of the UN who would transmit copies to the Economic and Social Council for consideration and also to specialised agencies. The Council may transmit the report to Human Rights Commission for recommendations (Article 19), to other organs of the UN, their subsidiary organs and specialised agencies concerned with furnishing technical assistance. (Article 22). The Council may also submit to the General Assembly the reports with recommendations of a general nature and a summary of the information received from the state parties.

The Covenant on Civil and Political Rights consists of a Preamble and 53 Articles divided into six parts. Recognising the inherent dignity, equal and inalienable rights of human beings as the foundation of freedom, justice and peace in the world, the Covenant requires the signatory states to respect and to ensure to all individuals within its territory, the rights mentioned in the Covenant. The State party undertakes to ensure to all persons 'effective remedy' against violation of their rights or freedom notwithstanding that the violation has been 'committed by persons acting in an official capacity'. The right to remedy shall be determined by competent judicial, administrative or legislative authority provided for, by the legal system of the state and wherever such remedy is granted, it shall be enforced by competent authorities (Article 3 a,b,c,). Part III describes the civil and political rights, such as, right to life, protection against torture or cruel inhuman or degrading treatment or punishment, right to liberty and security of person, equality before the courts and tribunals, right to freedom of thought, conscience and religion, right to hold opinion without interference, right to freedom of association and of peaceful assembly. According to Article 27, persons belonging to minorities in the state 'shall not be denied the right, in community with other members of their group, to enjoy their own culture, to process and practise their own religion or use their own language'.

In spite of providing a long list of civil and political rights, Article 4 contains a 'derogation clause' which empowers the States to derogate from their obligations in times of 'officially proclaimed' emergency which threatens the life of the nation to the extent strictly required by the exigencies of the situation. However, even under such situation a State cannot deprive anyone of life arbitrarily nor subject anyone to torture, cruel inhuman treatment or punishment, nor for that matter hold anyone in servitude.

We have seen that these two Covenants provide for different sets of rights, the common point being that both the Covenants have included the right of self-determination in Article I, thereby implying the importance attached to this right, albeit a controversial one. According to Article 1 of the Covenants "All people have the right of self-determination. By virtue of that right they freely determine their political status and freely pursue their economic, social and cultural development. Article 1(3) reads : 'the State parties to the present Covenant shall promote the realisation of the right of self-determination and shall respect that right in conformity with the provision of the Charter of the United Nations. It is left to the country concerned to determine the mechanisms for realising this right. The General Assembly considered this right as a pre-requisite to the full enjoyment of all human rights. Nonetheless, this right has been subjected to a number of interpretations. Immediately after the Second World War, when fight against colonialism had gained momentum, this right provided succor to the colonised people to free themselves from the yoke of colonialism, in that this was interpreted as the right to gain independence from colonial rule and also racist regime. Decolonisation, however, meant freedom from the colonies without realignment of boundaries which could, otherwise have restored many units to the pre-colonial position. The

Declaration of Decolonisation (1960) recognises the right of self-determination but finds 'any attempt at the partial or total disruption of the national unity and territorial integrity of a country as incompatible with the purposes and principles of the Charter of the UN. It further declares : 'all peoples have the right to self-determination and that by virtue of that right they freely pursue their economic social and cultural development'.[1] The UN General Assembly World Conference on Human Rights (1993) regarded the denial of the right of self-determination to be a violation of Human Rights and underlined the importance of the effective realisation of the right. In the same vein, it maintained that 'it should not, however, be construed as authorising or encouraging any action which would dismember or impair totally or in part the territorial integrity or political unity of sovereign and independent states conducting themselves in compliance with the principle of equal rights'.[2] This standpoint denies right of self-determination to any political unit of new independent states. Speaking about this right in relation to the indigenous people, a UN Sub-Commission on Prevention of Discrimination and Protection of Minorities, pointed out that self-governance is 'an inherent part of their cultural and legal heritage which has contributed to their cohesion and to the maintenance of their social and cultural tradition...self-determination, in its many forms is thus a basic pre-condition if indigenous peoples are to be able to enjoy their fundamental rights and determine their future while at the same time preserving, developing and passing on their specific ethnic identity to future generations'.[3]

Through various declarations what the UN has indicated is that exercise of right of self-determinations should not lead to change in the political contour of existing countries through dismemberment. However, it is the duty of the State to take effective measures for the development of the minorities within the countries as specified in the Article 27 of the International Covenant on Civil and Political Rights. They may also involve the recognition that minority cultures are entitled to protect themselves by placing limits on the incursion of outsiders and limits on their own members' choice about career, family, lifestyle, loyalty etc.[4] When the exercise of this right does not lead to dismemberment but to the integration with another State, the UN raises no objection, for example, integration of Cosos-keeling island with Australia in 1984[5] or for that matter integration of Sikkim with the Indian union in 1975.

III

India as a signatory party to the Universal Declaration and other Covenants is committed to the adoption and implementation of these provisions. The Indian Constitution bears sufficient testimony to the country's commitment to the rights of its citizens. Part III of the Indian Constitution details the different rights known as 'Fundamental Rights' guaranteed to its people. These are right to equality (Art. 14-18), right to freedom (Art. 19), protection in respect to conviction for offence (Art. 20), protection of life and personal liberty (Art. 21), protection against arrest and detention in certain cases (Art. 22), right against exploitation (Art. 23-24), right to freedom of religion (Art. 25-28), cultural and minority rights (Art. 29-30), right to constitutional remedies (Art. 32), right to remedies for enforcement of fundamental right (Art. 32 & 226). Under the Code of Criminal Procedure (Cr. P.C.) every citizen has right against arbitrary or illegal arrest, right to be released on bail, protection against cruel and inhuman treatment during investigation. In cases of custodial deaths, it is mandatory that the cause of death be enquired by a Magistrate, either instead of or in addition to the investigation held by a police officer. Under the right to benefit of doubt (Indian Evidence Act), it is for the prosecution to produce proof that the accused is guilty beyond doubt. It underlines the right of the accused to be presumed innocent till proven guilty.

Besides the above rights, another landmark in guaranteeing the right to the people is the promulgation of the Protection of Human Rights Act, 1993. It stipulates the constitution of National Human Rights Courts.[6]

The National Human Rights Commission consists of a chairperson who has been a Chief Justice of the Supreme Court, a Judge of the Supreme Court, a Chief Justice of High Court, and two members to be appointed from amongst persons having knowledge or practical experience in matters relating to human rights [Sec. 3 (2)]. The State Human Rights Commission is to be constituted on similar lines with a chairperson who has been a Chief Justice of a High Court, one member who is, or has been a District Judge in that state and two members to be appointed from amongst persons having knowledge of, or practical experience in matters relating to human Rights [Sec. 21 (2)]. According to the provisions of the Act, Human Rights Court may also be constituted. Instead of constituting a separate body, the state governments may specify for each district a court of sessions as Human

Rights courts with the concurrence of the Chief Justice of the High Court (Sec. 30). For conducting cases in that court, the state government may appoint a public prosecutor or an advocate who has been in practice as an advocate for not less than seven years as a special public prosecutor (Sec. 31).

The Commission is empowered to enquire into violation of human rights and abetment thereof, negligence in the prevention of such violation by a public servant, intervene in any proceeding involving any allegation of violation of human rights pending before a court with the approval of such court, review the safeguards provided for the protection of Human Rights and recommend measures for their effective implementation.

Besides these, the Commission is expected to make recommendation for the effective implementation of treaties and international instruments on Human Rights, spread Human Rights literacy among various sections of society and promote awareness of the safeguards available for the protection of these rights and encourage the NGOs and other institutions in the field of Human Rights. (Sec. 12).

The nature of functions assigned to the Human Rights Commission shows that they are empowered to enquire into the violation of Human Rights, to review the safeguards provided for the protection of Human Rights, and to recommend measures for their effective implementation, and review the factors, including acts of terrorism, that inhibit the enjoyment of human rights, and recommend appropriate measures. In order to ensure that the people are protected against violation, the Commission can enquire into the violation *suo motu* or on the basis of a petition presented to it by the victim or any person on his behalf and also spread human rights awareness among the people through seminars, etc. and encourage the works of the NGOs working in the field.

From the above discussion, it is evident that the Human Rights of the citizens have been sufficiently guaranteed under the Constitution and different Acts. The constitution of Human Rights Commission and a number of functions assigned to it is another important step towards protecting the people against any atrocities committed by the government machinery. In spite of all these, what has been India's record of fulfilling these objectives ? India is known internationally to champion the rights of the states fighting against colonialism and recist regime but at the same time it is one such country which has been confronting the autonomy claims raised by various groups. The demand for secession is based either on historical antecedent or ethnic identities.

How has India been tackling the problem? What is its record of ensuring human rights to the people of such regions?

IV

The political history of NE India since the Independence is replete with aspirations of various ethnic groups to carve out a niche for themselves outside the Indian Union. The core issue in this imbroglio is the exercise of the right of self-determination in that the different groups leading the autonomy movements have projected India as a colonial power. It is argued that Assam had never been a part of India till the implementation of the Treaty of Yandaboo (1826), that Manipur had its own constitution till 1947 and was an independent state till its merger with the Indian Union in 1949. Nagaland's claim to separation is also based on historical facts and that the state had never been a part of British India.[7]

The consistent stand of the Government of India is that the right of self-determination applied only to the people under foreign domination and did not apply to sovereign independent states or to a section of people or nations—which is the essence of national integrity.[8] Naturally, its policy towards the NE since the Independence is characterized by carrot and stick policy. On the one hand, in a bid to contain the volatile situation, separate states were carved out on linguistic basis. Thus, out of Assam emerged the states of Maghalaya, Nagaland, Mizoram and union territories upgraded to full fledged states. Political and cultural integrity is sought to be achieved by envisaging non-discriminatory provisions in the Constitution. Under the VIth Schedule of the Constitution, provisions have been made for the constitution of autonomous hill councils whereby the people have been granted powers to plan for the development of the region as per the local needs. The North Eastern Council has been constituted with this end in view.

On the other hand, India views violence by the groups spearheading the liberation movements as acts of terrorism and wide ranging powers have been given to the army and paramilitary forces like CRPF, BSF, Assam Rifles and state police under various special powers Acts to tackle the so called menance of terrorism. The Acts under which these forces draw powers are the Assam Disturbed Act, 1955; the Armed Forces Special Powers Act, 1958 which was later amended and named North East Armed Forces (Special Power) Act, 1972; Assam

Maintenance of Public Order, 1953; Nagaland Security Regulation, 1962 etc. Although, these Acts envisage the role of armed forces strictly as that of aiding civil administration, whenever and wherever they have been deployed they have taken over the power of civil administration instead, as was seen in the Operation Blue Bird, Rhino I & II, Tiger Heart etc.[9] These Acts give security forces wide powers such as, to resort to indiscriminate mass raids [10], to arrest and detain[11], power to shoot to kill[12] and immunity from prosecution[13]. The tactics adopted by them is same everywhere *i.e.* to instil fear psychosis in the minds of the people and dislocate normal life by resorting to physical torture, indiscriminate killing, wanton searches and arrests, etc.[14]

While submitting the second periodic report to the Human Rights Committee, United Nations in 1991, India defended the Special Powers Act on two grounds: (1) army gained such authority in view of the disturbed situation in a particular area and (2) that India had reasons to believe that agitation in certain border states was being aided and abetted by foreign elements infiltrating into Indian territory and stringent measures became necessary in order to protect innocent people from being killed by terrorists.[15] Such a position implies that principles of freedom, justice, rights and peace are to be determined by the State and it can take any step in the name of providing these to the people, thereby maintaining its hegemony over the region. In this context, it appears that the State and law in sanctioning compliance with rights are without question justified in using force, if necessary, little realising that these actions infringe upon the people's right to be human.[16]

The use of force by the Government in order to ensure the rights of the people and to maintain its territorial integrity and sovereignty has resulted in a long drawn fight between the security forces and the insurgents. Whether the measures adopted so far have led to the integration of the people with the national mainstream or to the alienation of the people needs to be reflected upon.

There is recorded evidence to show that empowered by the Special Powers Acts, the security forces have committed heinous crimes on the public infringing people's rights and liberties that are enshrined in the Constitution. One positive contribution of such state of affairs is the peoples' resolution to fight against oppression and injustices. A number of Human Rights Organisations such as Naga People's Movement for Human Rights (NPMHR) and Imphal based Civil Liberties and Human Rights Organisation (CLAHRO), Manab Adhikar Sangram Samiti (MASS) have been formed. These organisations not only seek to educate and mobilise people against injustice but also seek constitutional redressal in case of violation of humanrights.

The NPMHR was formed in September, 1978 'in response to Naga people's long felt need for an organised movement to protect and further HR which have been trampled by the Indian military since Independence in 1947'.[17] Immediately after its formation the Association organised the Human Rights Week in Nagaland from December 10-15, 1978. During the week, its workers toured villages and held public meetings. In these meetings, problems of human rights violations were debated upon intensively, and cases of violation were also reported. In November, 1990, the Organisation represented some cases of violation of HR committed by the Assam Rifles personnel to the Government of Nagaland. The brutality of the forces can be gauged from the fact that in October 1990 most of the Northern Angami village comprising of 8-10 villages were subjected to inhuman treatment by the Assam Rifles personnel. Besides innocent people, high officials of the Government of Nagaland including the Home Secretary were harassed and humiliated. The official car of the Minister for Power was shot at, his body-guard disarmed at gun point and the minister made to stand with hands up for three hours. This was allegedly done in retaliation against the ambush of Assam Rifles personnel on October, 12, 1990. The directives of the Chief Secretary, Government of Nagaland to the Inspector General, Assam Rifles and the DIG, Assam Rifles, Nagaland range to stop harassment and ill treatment of innocent persons as 'these would not help in isolating the elements indulging in unlawful activities' was not heeded upon.[18] The NPMHR have also moved a number of petitions of *Habeas Corpus* in the Gauhati High Court on behalf of the victims of such violations.[19]

The same story of army atrocities is repeated in Manipur, where army was deployed in September, 1979, after it was declared a disturbed area. The Armed Forces (Assam & Manipur) Special Powers Act was extended to the whole of the state.[20] Since then the state witnessed brutality committed by paramilitary and armed forces under the names of different operations. These operations were generally conducted by the security forces in retaliation against attacks on its personnel by insurgents. Under such operations, village after village was subjected to inhuman torture leading to dislocation of normal life, fear psychosis and, in extreme cases, to deaths of victims. As for example, the Singjamei operation was conducted in retaliation against an attack on army jawans, the Patsoi operation in retaliation against the killing of three CRPF personnel by the insurgents, the infamous Oinam operation (Operation Blue Bird) in retaliation against an attack on the Assam Rifles personnel by a group of insurgents belonging to the NSCN.[21]

A detailed report on the Oinam operation was prepared by the Amnesty International (AI) entitled 'India. Operation Blue Bird'. The operation resulted in torture and extra-judicial execution. The AI made a number of recommendations to the Government of India.[22]

Like in Nagaland, in Manipur, Civil Liberties and Human Rights Organisation (CLAHRO) has been working to restore democracy and the rule of law wherein the life and security of the citizens could be guaranteed. It also took leading part in assisting common people for taking legal actions in cases of death in army custody and disappearance. Not only has it challenged the imposition of the 'Armed Forces Special Powers Act, 1985', but it also insisted on the Central Government to introduce a mandatory provision of law for issuing "Arrest Memo" in respect of persons arrested by police and other security forces.[23]

The activities of the security forces deployed in the NE indicate a flagrant violation of the Article 3 of the Universal Declaration of Human Rights which states 'everyone has the right to life, liberty and security of person'. Even the 'derogation clause' (Article 4) of the Covenant on Civil and Political Rights which empowers the states to derogate from obligation in times of "officially proclaimed" emergency specifies that the state cannot deprive anyone of life arbitrarily nor subject anyone to torture, cruel, inhuman treatment or punishment. Though there is no dearth of provisions in the Constitution guaranteeing the people freedom and justice, the incidents of alleged paramilitary and military excesses are not infrequent. The reports of missing persons, molestation, torture, unlawful confinement do not speak well for a country which prides in calling itself the biggest democracy in the world and which does not hesitate to speak against colonialism, racism in international fora.

The practical compulsion of keeping its political boundary unaltered has overshadowed the ethical question of right or wrong, though the concept of HR is as much a political issue as an ethical one. The target of the government policy is to achieve the socio-cultural integration of the people of NE region with the Indian polity, but as events show, it has at best succeeded in alienating the people and has reinforced the idea of Indian colonialism.

The Universal Declaration, Covenants, Instruments and resolutions of the UN have always held out hopes to the oppressed people of the world. Various ethnic groups claiming autonomy interpret the right of self-determination as the solution to their problem. The UN, in spite of guaranteeing this right in two important Covenants, have always upheld the territorial integrity and sovereignty of a country. Thus, the realisation of the goal by such groups depends on the desire of the state authority.

More than half a century has passed since the adoption of the Universal Declaration of Human Rights, but it still remains a central challenge to civilisation. This is due to the fact that the onus of implementing the UN provisions on Human Rights lies with the signatory states. These states discharge the responsibility within the country's political parameters and available resources. The violation of HR in the NE India can be contained through the political will of the authority, the spread of human rights literacy among the people and its own administrators. The Human Rights Commission and different organisations like NPMHR, CLAHRO, MASS can play an effective role in this regard. Among the different functions, the Human Rights Commission is empowered to enquire into violation of human rights and abetment thereof, negligence in the prevention of such violation by a public servant, intervene in any proceeding involving any allegation of violation of human rights pending before a court, review the safeguard provided for the protection of human rights and recommend measures for their effective implementation. In these, it is seen, that the Commission has a role to play only after the violation has been committed but most important it is to prevent such violation at the first instant itself. This can be achieved if the two designated functions are taken in earnest, *i.e.* (1) to spread human right literacy among various sections of society and promote awareness of safeguards available for the protection of these rights through publications, mass media, seminar and other available means and (2) to encourage the efforts of non-governmental organisations and institutions working in the field of human rights. The Charter and the Constitution may underline the duty of the State to ensure human rights to its citizens, but ultimately it is the peoples' power which will act as a safeguard against any abuse of power.

NOTES AND REFERENCES

1. V.T. Thamilmaran : *Human Rights in Third World Perspective,* New Delhi, Har-Anand, 1992. p. 196.
2. "United Nations General Assembly World Conference on Human Rights Vienna Declaration and Programme of Action", June 1993 in Naorem

Sanajaoba (Ed) *Human Rights Principle, Practices & Abuses, Annexure VI,* New Delhi Omsons Publications, p. 283.

3. *Quoted in* S. James Anaya "The Capacity of International Law to Advance Ethnic or Nationality Rights claims" in Will Kymlicka (Ed) : *The Rights of Minority Cultures,* OUP, 1995, p. 325.
4. Jeremy Waldron : "Minority Cultures and Cosmopolitan Alternative" in Will Kymlicka, *ibid.*, p. 97.
5. I.A. Shearer : *Starke's International Law,* London, Butterworths, 1994, p. 113.
6. *The Protection of Human Rights Act,* 1993, Gazette of India, Extra, Part II, Section I, dt. 10th January, 1994, pp. 1-16.
7. Naorem Sanajaoba : "Right of Nations to Self-Determination (Principles and Practices) in Naorem Sanajaoba (ed) *op. cit.* p. 54.
8. Paramjit S. Jaswal & Nishtha Jaswal : *Human Rights and the Law,* New Delhi, APH Pub. Corporation, 1996, p. 347.
9. (a) MASS : "Human Rights Violation in Assam (Operations Rhino 1991)", pp. 137-172.
   (b) Kshireswar Borah : "Human Rights Violation in Assam" pp. 277-281.
   (c) Neingulo Krome : "Human Rights Movement in Nagaland" pp. 173-178.
   (d) N. Nimai Singh : "Human Rights Abuses by Security Forces in Manipur" pp. 179-193.

   9.a-d are included in Naorem Sanajaoba (ed) *op. cit.*
10. Section 4(d) of the (Assam) Armed Forced Special Powers Act empowers commissioned officer, warrant officer, NGO or any other person of equivalent rank in Armed Forces 'to enter' and search without warrant, any premises, to make any such arrest.
11. Section 4(c) of the Act gives a commissioned officer, a warrant officer, a NCO or other ranking officer power to arrest without warrant, any person who has committed a cognisable offence or against whom a reasonable suspicion exists that he has committed or is about to commit a cognisable offence.
12. Section 4(a) of the Act empowers a commissioned officer, a warrant officer, a NCO or any person of equivalent rank in the armed forces, if he believes it necessary to do so for the maintenance of public order, power to fire upon or otherwise use force even to the causing of death against any person who is acting in contravention of any law or order for the time being in force in the disturbed area prohibiting the assembly of five or more persons or the carrying of weapons or of things capable of being used as weapons and of five arms ammunition or explosive substances.
13. Section 6 of Act reads "No prosecution suit or other legal proceeding shall be instituted except with the previous sanction of the central government,

against any person in respect of anything done or purported to be done in exercise of the powers conferred by this (mentioned above) Act".

14. N. Nimai Singh, *op. cit.,* p. 179.
15. "Report of the Human Rights Committee, United Nations, 1991, India" in Naorem Sanajaoba (ed) *op. cit.,* Annexure III, p. 253.
16. Upendra Baxi : *Inhuman Wrongs and Human Rights: Unconventional Essays,* New Delhi, Har-Anand, 1994, pp. 1-17.
17. Neingulo Krome, O*p. cit.,* p. 173.
18. *Ibid.,* pp. 175-76.
19. *Ibid.,* pp. 177-78.
20. N. Nimai Singh, O*p. cit.,* pp. 268-76.
21. *Ibid.,* p. 186-90.
22. For details see, Naorem Sanajaoba, *op. cit..* pp. 268-76.
23. N. Nimai Singh, *op. cit.,* pp. 192.

3

Human Rights Education

An Integrated Approach

N.B. Biswas

All great human civilisations have been concerned about human rights in some way or the other. The Greeks developed a notion of the 'natural law' according to which, each being had its own inherent value. In the West, the thought has evolved through revolutionary events beginning with enactments like the Magna Carta (1215), the Bill of Rights (1669), the Habeas Corpus Act (1670), Rights of Petition (1628) the Virginia Declaration of Rights (1776), Declaration of Rights of Man and Citizen of France (1889), Hague Conventions (1899 and 1907), the Treaty of Versailles (1919) and so on. In India, it is found in the writings of persons like Ram Mohan Roy, Mahatma Gandhi, Jawahar Lal Nehru, B.R. Ambedkar, M. N. Roy, Ram Manohar Lohia and others.

The internationalisation of human rights was begun by the League of Nations after the World War I. The allied countries of the World War II, too ascertained to preserve human rights and justice in their own lands as well as in other countries. The United Nations which was formed in 1945 stated, 'to achieve international co-operation in promoting and encouraging respect for human rights and for fundamental freedom for all without distinction as to race, sex, language or religion'. The Universal Declaration of Human Rights was the outcome of this resolve in the form of an International Bill of Rights of June 1946 adopted as the Declaration on December 10, 1948. The United Nations again adopted the Declaration of the Rights of the Child, on November 20, 1959 in order to protect children.

The Universal Declaration of Human Rights was a milestone in judicial and human history as it embodied a set of guarantees for a person to be able not only to live but to live with dignity in order to develop fully and use one's human qualities, intelligence, talents and conscience to satisfy one's spiritual, physical, social and other needs. The Declaration affirmed one's right to be human.

Decades have passed, but the world scenario today presents a dismal picture of human rights. India, particularly the North-Eastern part of it has a record of flagrant violation of Human Rights. A wide range of conflicts in the socio-cultural and the political arena threatens the rights of a very large number of people in North-East India. The very fabric of Indian society is disrupted by the perpetuation of different conflict situations centering inter-religious and inter-ethnic questions and sub-nationalistic assertions. On the other hand, the outcome of the arbitrary acts of successive governments, like illegal detentions, mindless killings in encounters, torture, rape and deaths in custody are only a few illustrations among the situations which find regular mention in Amnesty International Report. The list is incomplete if a mention is not made of discrimination against women, untouchables, tribals, 'dalits' and bonded labour and child labour practised openly on an extensive scale. Very often, such open violation is not only accepted and tolerated, but even enforced along with the public authorities themselves participating in it. It is no wonder, then, that such a state-of-affairs exists, for, every reform, law and legislation is replete with loopholes.

Against the backdrop of this utter violation of human rights certain questions need to be posed:

i) Why the human rights are violated?
ii) How is the very concept of human rights understood in the socio-political and cultural perspective of North-East India?
iii) Can education, especially human rights education contribute a significant addendum to awareness in this regard?
iv) What kind of approach may be formulated in turning violence into peace through human rights education?

An attempt should be made to find out answers to the above questions. In the first section of the article I present a general review of the human rights. The second section deals with the implication of human rights in the Indian Context which is followed by an analysis of the concept of Human Rights Education. The last section presents the strategies and approaches for turning violence into peace through Human Rights Education in North East India.

I. General Review of the Human Rights

When the English barons forced King John to accede to the Magna Carta in 1215, they launched a historical process that continues to the present day: ruling elites were compelled to accept limits on their exercise of power in order to protect the rights of the people. While the barons used the threat of civil war to induce King John to seal their articles, the Universal Declaration of Human Rights was the indirect result of zealous lobbying by thousands of individuals and non-governmental groups at the United Nations Conference on International Organisation (UNCIO) in San Francisco, which ended on June 26, 1945 with the signing of the UN Charter.

In his 1941 "Four Freedoms Speech" President Roosevelt proclaimed that "freedom of speech, freedom of worship, freedom from want, and freedom from fear" were "the necessary conditions of peace". World War II provided abundant evidence of the failure of earlier peace-keeping efforts and led to calls for the creation of a post-war security organisation to succeed the League of Nations. In this setting 46 states signed the Declaration of the UN in January, 1942. As the war drew to an end in 1944, the "Big Four Powers" (US, UK, USSR, and China) met at Dumbarton Oaks to work out an agreement on the shape of this new organisation; and at Yalta in February, 1945 Roosevelt, Churchill and Stalin resolved their differences on procedures and representation.

The topic of human rights was not prominent in any of these discussions and the term "human rights" was not used in the covenant of the League of Nations. Early drafts of the UN Charter did contain a bill of rights, but most states were reluctant to compromise their sovereignty by binding themselves to such articles as a condition of UN membership. By most accounts, the representatives of the 50 nations thought that there were too many interpretations of "human rights" to allow consensus. The fact that human rights were placed on the San Fransico agenda, and that the resulting Charter committed UN members to "promote universal respect for, and observance of human rights and fundamental freedoms for all without distinction as to race, sex, language, or religion," is generally credited to the efforts of the "people's delegates", the thousands of individuals and representatives of non-governmental organisations who scrutinised and influenced the conference delegates.

Mandated to create an international bill of rights, the UN Economic and Social Council (UNESCO) established a Human Rights Commission, chaired by Eleanor Roosevelt. The Commission was charged with drafting a document to accommodate the diverse political and economic systems and cultures of UN member states. In early 1947, responding to criticism that her initial three-member drafting committee had been given too much power with too little representation, Eleanor Roosevelt engineered a compromise. A drafting committee of eight (Australia, Chile, China, France, Lebanon, UK, US and USSR) was to work from a "documented outline" prepared by the Human Rights Division of the UN Secretariat.

The text of the Universal Declaration now reads ""'All human beings are born free and equal in dignity and rights. They are endowed with reason toward one another in a spirit of brotherhood."

In September 1948, the Human Rights Commission passed its draft of the Universal Declaration to the General Assembly's Third Committee (on Social, Cultural and Humanitarian Questions), which devoted 81 meetings to the Declaration and considered 168 amendments. The most hotly debated articles were Art. 18, on freedom of thought, conscience and religion.

On the evening of December 10, 1948, it was unanimously passed by the General Assembly, though eight countries (USSR, Czechoslovakia, Byelorussia, Yugoslavia, Poland, Ukraine, Saudi Arabia, and South Africa) abstained.

The historical process which began with the Magna Carta, was resumed in San Francisco. The process goes on to this day, and it must continue until all people enjoy all of the rights which are justly 'ours'.

II. Implication of HR in Indian Context and HR Education

What do all these efforts in their historical contexts mean to us, to multicultural framework of education and to our very own survival as members of the human family? The concept of human dignity should lie at the heart of every educational pursuit dealing with multiplicity of culture, and diverse socio-political and historical perspectives. Creation of a social order attuned to this day and age is the target of such pursuit. The process of preserving and sustaining human dignity is analogous to what we strive for in the struggle for equality among ethnic groups. It should help us to understand and learn how to make society liveable from a realistic standpoint. Such a society would be humane and guarantee a quality of life that not only enriches the human spirit but also preserves and sustains a healthy environment.

The approach in establishing the relationship of Human Rights Education to Multicultural Education is holistic. This approach is viewed as consistent with the ecological principles or whole system of thought and thinking that are emerging as paradigms most appropriate to the formation of planetary citizens. Holism when applied to Human Rights Education interprets all rights and entitlements as interrelated and interdependent components of human dignity.

Essential to the holistic approach to human rights education is community education. The concept of community has been at the heart of the process of humanising this multicultural society that we share. It is only when we realise that we live with each other and for each other that we can embrace the concept of community. It is the feeling of being part of a community *vis-a-vis* the human family that can transform us from the selfish individual and power centered domination into the community. This power driven divisiveness as we see it in Bosnia, Somalia, South Africa and in many part of the world including the United States has to stop because it reduces the dignity of the "subject people", the most tragic of which is thc subjugation of children and women to the most painful experience of the cruelty. It is clearly the failure of the human mind that we fail to honour as a code of behaviour, which since time immemorial provided guidance to a better life in this planet. The value of community and helping one another is one quality that can preserve human dignity and social order amidst continuing struggle for equality and freedom.

Indian society, specially the society in North East India is not spared from the painful cry of recapturing a sense of community because of the increasing crime and violence mostly due to racial tensions and ethnic/cultural differences or conflict. The sense of community is increasingly being viewed as the essential cure for the alienation of one community from another.

The parameters of Human Rights Education in this article include (1) a historical perspective, (2) the impact of human rights/human dignity on ethnic groups, women, children and other segments of society such as those with special needs, (3) sample teaching strategies for uplifting human dignity in a multicultural society utilising important documents such as the Universal Declaration of Human Rights (United Nations), Bill of Rights (United States), The Rights of the Child, International Women's Rights and others that are included in the Chronology of Human Rights Agreements. It will utilise Educating for Human Dignity: Learning About Rights and Responsibilities : A K-12 Teaching Resource as an example of a primary text book in Human Rights Education. This will help to develop the concept of a peaceful living in a civil society. The concept of a civil society brings us to the heart of human rights education which we can achieve with a degree of success if we can accept each other as human beings and concretise it with a manner of behaving that is civil and decent not violent but peaceful. This brings us to the culture of peace which UNESCO Director General, Federico Mayor has often spoken of in his numerous speeches as representative of the world body, the United Nations. According to Mayor, "the culture of peace is impossible without the culture of democracy. And democracy is not a value system and set of behaviour which can be exported pre-packaged and ready for consumption like a Big Mac. All of us must speak from the complexities of creating democracy and the need to begin with three essential elements : freedom of the press and media, free speech and an independent judiciary. From these roots tolerance of political fair play can eventually grow up but no transfer of the American or any other system should be expected to take roots in cultures that have their own histories and specificities".

The legacy of Human Rights Education to Multicultural Education is a global concept which together with the three R's is evolving as the *Fourth R in Education.* A new publication of Amnesty International USA's National Steering Committee on Human Rights Education which started in the fall of 1988 was entitled : *Human Rights Education : The Fourth R.* Its preface stated "the title of this bulletin, *Human Rights Education : The Fourth R* derives from our belief that the teaching of human rights is as basic as the teaching of the traditional three R's. *The Fourth R* should occupy a central place in the school curriculum as reading, writing and arithmetic. It is essential for a global understanding of multiculturalism as we welcome the twenty first century. Indeed it is as important as the 3R's if not more important as we realise more and more that we are brothers and sisters in this struggle to preserve human dignity, integrity and equality. Who are we after all without human dignity?"

Human Rights Education

The World Conference of Human Rights considers human rights education, training and public information and achievement of stable and harmonious relations among communities and for fostering mutual understanding, tolerance and peace. States should strive to eradicate illiteracy and should direct education towards the full development of the human personality and to the strengthening of respect for human rights and fundamental freedoms. The World Conference on Human Rights calls on all states and institutions to include human rights, humanitarian law, democracy and rule of law as subjects in the curricula of all learning situations in formal and non-formal settings. Human rights education should include peace, democracy, development and social justice, as set forth in international and regional human rights instruments, in order to achieve common understanding and awareness with a view to strengthening universal commitment to human rights.

III. Strategies for Education

Education for human rights need to be an important value at every level of life and in particular of our educational system. Values are the determinants in a human person that influence his/her choice in life and thus decide behaviour. In the absence of values related to human person the dignity of the human being gets trodden underfoot.

This brings the need of a more relevant curriculum relating to the life-needs or experiences of an individual. According to Dr. D. H. Worth "to meet the challenge of the relevance...requires the identification and provision of the opportunity for certain activities and experiences, that are systematically linked with the world of work". Most students do not want merely to accumulate factual knowledge. They want to work at something in which they are interested, something which they perceive significant to their personal lives. Educational Institutions are the most appropriate places where the value of 'humanness' of human dignity is fully expanded and where the education for human rights becomes realistic and concrete.

Concern for the development of the values related to human rights, prompted teacher educators to evolve a few strategies for adoption, in secondary schools. It is one's fond hope that these approaches and strategies will provide an awareness leading to action on human rights through the curriculum of the secondary schools in India.

Strategy one : Institutional objectives reflecting the concern for human rights

Education for human rights should be all pervasive and largely developed through a conscious effort. The objectives spelt out by the institution in this light get a new direction and emphasis, influencing the teaching-learning process. These objectives once evolved, could be the basis for an Action Plan to plan and implement strategies for Human Rights Awareness through the curriculum. The following guidelines and procedure would be of assistance for the development of awareness on human rights and rights of the child, through the institutional objectives.

Phase I: Identification of Human Rights Components

Step 1: Orientation

i) The staff members are given an orientation on the thrust of the institution on safeguarding human rights, and are guided to identify the components related to human rights/rights of the child, in the objectives of the institution and to follow the procedure of this strategy, in their respective classrooms.

ii) At the commencement of the academic year, the students are given a general orientation on human rights, familiarised with the Declarations, emphasising these as the thrust of the institution and are motivated to perceive them in the context of their school curriculum and cocurricular activities.

Step 2: Brainstorming Session

Under the guidance of the class-teacher, the students of each class identify 'values' related to human rights in the objectives of the institution, *e.g.*, concern, respect for others etc.

Step 3: Categorisation of values on Human Rights

From the entire list of specific values identified, the students are helped to club together specific values related to each other, into broad-based categories of Human Rights Values, e.g., there may be one or two broad-based categories like Respect, Freedom etc.

Step 4: Operational Definition

The broad-based values are defined operationally to facilitate the concrete action plan, *e.g.*, respect for a person could be operationally defined as graciousness in our dealings with others, seeing other's points of view, including them in our circle of friends and so on.

Phase II: Preparation of the Action Plan

Step 1: Aspects of Human Rights Components

The teacher helps the students to pick out specific components on human rights related to the broad-based human rights value and clarifies each concretely, *e.g.*, the component 'graciousness in our dealings with others' is clarified in terms of the concrete meanings of the word 'graciousness' and 'others'.

Step 2: Development of the Action Plan

The students are helped to indicate how each of these components/ qualities can be practised by them through the curriculum and co-curricular activities, *e.g.*, based on the lesson, 'Indian Democracy at Work', in the Social Studies text book of Std. IX, they identify the opportunities available to 'listen to the points of view of others'. A number of specific, concrete, measurable action plan statements are worked out on the different components of the broad-based value. These could include programmes, projects, field trips and just personal activities.

Step 3: Implementation of the Action Plan

The class finalises the action plan, which can be put up in the classroom as a reminder for implementation during the year.

Step 4: Review of the Action Plan

Periodic review can be taken up, perhaps once a month, to share their experiences of practising their action plan. This is an aid towards internalisation of the spirit of human rights. A final review could be made at the end of the year. A rating scale could be prepared to study the extent of their effort towards practising the action plan. The review could be at the class level as well as school level.

The above strategy can bring about a personal attitudinal change as well as institutional transformation in terms of commitment to human rights.

Strategy two : Human rights through the integrated approach

While institutional objectives are an entry-point in making the curriculum experience oriented in terms of human rights, the syllabi/ course contents, which form a part of the curriculum, or the text books at the secondary school level are a major source of providing this learning experience. The text books at the school level are prepared by the Education Department of the State Governments. Teaching of the subjects involves not merely the passing on of information contained in the lesson under 3tudy, but even more importantly inducing in the students certain qualities of mind and heart in its learning. One such quality is developing a sense of safeguarding rights of every human person.

Values, including those related to human rights are also embedded in the content of a lesson. Classroom teacher should be trained to analyse the content and identify these values at certain points of significance. At that point of time the teacher can highlight the value identified and use techniques to help the students to consider it, clarify the issue and personalise the value related to human rights. This point where the value identified can be given emphasis for personalisation through the process of integration into the content, is termed as the 'plug point'. The strategy for integrating the personalisation of human rights components with the curriculum using 'plug points' can have the following format.

Phase I: Identification of the Human Rights Components at a Plug Point in a Lesson

As specified above, the teacher studies the text book and locates lessons which cater to human rights education. The content of the lesson is analysed as teaching point and the human rights components are identified at a plug point *e.g.,* the lesson, 'India and the World' in the Social Studies text book for Std. X, specifically deals with the United Nations Organisations and highlights the aims of the UNO, one being, 'to promote respect for human rights, dignity and freedom'. This is identified as a plug point.

Phase II: Framing Instructional Objectives of the Value of Human Rights Identified

The teacher, for instance, identifies the plug point on Gandhiji's philosophy of action to fight oppression and racial discrimination, in the lesson on Freedom Movement, in Std. X Social Studies text book. A specific instructional objective is framed e.g., 'to imbibe in the students the attitude of looking upon people of different castes, classes, religion and nationalities as brothers and sisters'

Phase III: Discussion and Action on the Human Rights Value Identified

After teaching the content of the teaching point upto the plug point, the teacher focuses through questioning or other eliciting techniques, on the human rights components. She spends time to guide the students to discuss its characteristics, needs and application to one's personal life. Various techniques can be adopted through the use of pictures, quotations, slogans, newspaper clipping, role plays, etc. It can even lead to a project with extension and community based activities. This could be the starting point of motivating the student to study the Declarations and to work on a project to implement its spirit in their own day to day living as well as make specific commitments towards promoting the spirit of human rights in their community.

The approach of integrating the components of human rights through syllabus is a powerful technique of personalising the values involved in the Declaration on Human Rights and the Rights of the Child.

Strategy three: Activities in education

Addressing the Thirty-third International Conference of the World Education Fellowship, 1986-87, Bombay Chapter, Dr. James Hemming described that the very survival of human-kind, animal-kind and plant-kind depends on an increase in caring—caring for others, caring for what is beautiful, caring for all life, caring for the plants, caring for our environment and caring for the future. The education of this caring impulse would imply the development of the capacity for caring in the learner through the school milieu which encourages such a capacity. It demands a change towards humanising the curriculum process. This includes the qualities of sensitivity, empathy, emotional awareness, perception in relationship, preference for synthesis rather than analysis, on a top priority in the learning process.

A participant climate in a school makes a dull teaching shop into a caring society and a caring world. The curriculum that is oriented towards the fostering of such a caring impulse will provide the 'heart' to the education of the learners. Schools that provide the 'heart' of education, make it meaningful for a full and effective life which includes the mastery of the basic skills, development of social attitudes and personal qualities, thus mobilising the child's total potentialities and widening the socialising and humanising experience.

A caring person is a person who lives the spirit of human rights. An experience-based study could form an essential part of this 'caring environment'. Some techniques for such a study are listed below:

1. Activity workshops to depict the articles of the Declarations through colleges, collection of newspaper cuttings to illustrate respect for or negation of human rights, slogans for application of human rights to life, log books or scrap books of quotations

and sayings, to strengthen human rights, and the like. Group activities by its very nature have an added dimension of developing the sprit of give and take, sharing, respect for one another and listening to the views of others.

2. Literary and Humanities club activities of elocution, composition of poems, essays for the wall magazine and school magazine, bulletin board displays, quizzing, role plays, based on the Declarations.
3. Extension education through awareness trekking on the theme of human rights, interviewing activities and social workers in this field, twinning with children's groups or schools deprived of basic amenities of life, living through camp programmes for exposure to such situations, can provide true living experiences.

IV. Process of turning Violence into Peace

The United Nations Peace Council, had started a movement in the name of 'Atoms for Peace' in the United States as early as 1960. Education for teenagers in our secondary schools, needs to be strengthened through a movement, 'Atoms of Love'. Unless the atoms of love explode and spread through the education of our children, during their developmental years, we will end up with a society in which large number of people lack humanitarian vision and concern. This is the responsibility of secondary school education which can capitalise on the tremendous power of adolescent idealism and energy.

It is heartening to note that suddenly the authorities of the country and media have woken up and open discussions on avoiding violence are made all over the country. The menace of violence among our boys and girls is no less serious and indeed it is an evil in our institutional life. Through our indifference we are slowly developing an insensitive attitude towards violence which eats into the vitals of educational institution. All our efforts are necessary to combat such evils from the educational institution.

The UNO has also made an effort to bring the desirable changes among the youth for avoiding violence and to establish peace and harmony between peoples. The UN Human Rights documents reveal in its Declaration that "all means of education should foster the ideals of peace, humanity, liberty and international solidarity".

It is suggested that "young people shall be brought up in the knowledge of the dignity and equality of all men, without distinction as to race, colour, ethnic origins or beliefs. Exchange, travel, tourism, meetings, the study of foreign language, the twinning of towns and universities without discrimination should be encouraged."

Further the declaration on the Elimination Of All Forms Of Intolerance assured that "the child shall be protected from any form of discrimination on the grounds of religion or belief. He shall be brought up in a spirit of understanding, tolerance, friendship among peoples, peace and universal brotherhood, respect for freedom of religion and belief of others, and in full consciousness that his energy and talents should be developed."

Education at all levels should be democratised, so that the inner potentialities of the young learners can be liberated and their action as well as thought be relieved from collective psychoses and individual inertia. Their creative faculties can flourish only through freedom and ethical excellence.

The value of peace should be inculcated in the children of India. The acquisition of peace as a value should become an integral part of the socialisation which begins at home and extends to schools, community and nations. Mahatma Gandhi said, "If we are to reach real peace in this world and if we are to carry on a real war against war, we shall have to begin with children."

School children need to be educated on the importance of peace and peace making. The development of human society is ultimately built on and sustained by the value of peace imbibed by people during their formative years.

Peace marches, meetings and walks should be organised for the learners to proclaim every child's right to peace. Peace education should be imparted to all school children. And that should include development of knowledge, skills and attitudes for the realisation of a human and peaceful world. The school should accept it as a social and moral obligation.

NOTES AND REFERENCES

Coombs, P. H. *The World Crisis in Education : The View from the Eighties*, New York : Oxford University, 1985.

Coomaraswamy, R. A. *Third World View of Human Rights.* UNESCO Courier, August/September, 1982.

Dougherty, J. *Materials for Teaching Human Rights in Secondary Schools.* Strasbourg : International Institute of Human Rights, 1984.

Deminguez, J.I., Nigel, S., Wood, B. *Enhancing Global Human Rights.* New York, McGraw Hill, 1979.

Humphrey, J. *Human Rights and the United Nations : A Great Adventure.* Dobbs Ferry, NJ : Transnational, 1984.

Human Rights Commission : *The Teaching of Human Rights, Paper No. 6,* Canberra, Australian Publishing Services, 1984.

Kneller, G. *Educational Anthropology : An Introduction,* New York : John Wiley and Sons, 1965.

Federico Mayor, *"Culture of Peace : Science Education and UNESCO"*, Iowa State University, Iowa, November 17, 1994.

Tarrow, N. B. *Human Rights and Education* (Ed.), New York : Pergamon Press, 1987.

UNESCO, *Proceeding of International Congress on the Teaching of Human Rights.* UNESCO, 1978.

II ~ Insurgency and Polity

4

Insurgency in the North East

Improving Awareness

Trigunesh Mukherjee

Historically, the region has proved to be rather prone to migration of people. Therefore, a tribal mix was a natural outcome. Added to this were the post 1947 migration and post 1971 movement of people from across the border under some pretext or the other. Yet, migration in recent times was accepted initially as convenient and cheap labour. Therefore, people who raise the "foreigners" issue should have acted then and not when they found the competition tough. One may add that even without migration this is nothing new in this region; "throw out the Bengals" or "liquidate the non-tribals or "throw out the foreigners (Indians not belonging to the region)" have been heard before. But currently the problem, specially in Assam, is acute because demographic patterns have been overhauled. Fear has also grown in people's hearts. No serious actions have been initiated because the same illegal migrants may have been the bulk but because of the linkage to power the same people can turn militant. Since religion is also at stake, fundamentalism can not be far behind. True, this does not hold good for all the states but understanding is necessary.

Non-involvement of the British, except where it concerned earnings, unfortunately was carried forward as policy even after the independence. Since Assam, in its original shape, looked after the whole of the North East—poor administration and lack of concern can be placed at their doorstep. Development did not take place, money supply was not evenly distributed and the plainsman exploited the hill people, mainly tribals. The seeds of unhappiness were easy to sow. There also was a growing perception of neglect and yet everyone wished to cling to "inner line" and linked problems. It would be clear, therefore, that irritants were in plenty even without going back in history. Since inertia in these States is very high it was convenient to externalise the problems—"The Centre is to blame".

Except in Nagaland, where armed conflict was an initial choice, all other States went through the cycle of appeals to administration, writing in the media, minor protests, massive strikes and so on. Ultimately, having lost patience they chose armed protest (or so it would seem).

The situation is quite complex because one is not really sure of the aims of militant groups and splinter groups. Yet, given the development (or lack of it) of communications, power, industries etc. massive protests would be a natural outcome. One cannot help but wonder and raise a few questions:—

(a) What has the region done for itself?

(b) Is there a strong element of "power seeking" by "individuals"?

(c) Was (is?) the administration effective and concerned?

(d) What specific improvements or developments have the militant groups carried out?

(e) Is there a 'will' to improve the status?

(f) Has too much (in terms of grants, aids, reservations, etc.) come too easily here?

(g) Is this a "law and order" problem?

Rate of implementation of Accords that have been signed is so poor that the Accords seem to have lost their way.

A brief look at the players (in an insurgency) is necessary:

- Government (both Central and State).
- Politicians.
- Administration.
- Police.
- NGO's
- Militant/Insurgent cadres and groups.
- Militant/Insurgent leaders (taken separately, because their lives today are quite dissimilar to that of the cadres they manipulate).
- Judiciary.
- Academics.
- Industry (Public and Private).
- Businessmen (capable of paying)

- Media.
- Para-Military Forces.
- The Army.

The Army

The Army's involvement in countering insurgency is indeed very intimate. It is, therefore, important for all the players to understand this unique organisation. People call for the Army whenever things go wrong; the masses are happy when the army is around and once the calamity is over they are forgotten, at least, by the authorities. Yet this organisation continues to deliver the goods all the time. As an aside, a representative of the current pay commission says the bureaucrats need to be better paid and looked after because of their experience and exposure, yet they are not particularly prominent in dealing with emergencies.

Insurgency is not a law and order problem though it goes through that stage in its evolution. One of the first premises is that the administrative machinery (including the police) was ineffective during the growth of insurgency. The second premise is that even earlier than the law and order stage insurgency was taking roots. The third premise is that a nascent stage also exists before the other two. Thoughts, ideas, plans, organisation *et al* are essential before an insurgency walk can be undertaken.

When is the Army Called. Analysis of all insurgencies will show that the Army is not called in at the "preventive" stage; they are called in at the "active" stage. In the meanwhile, a fair amount of abdication takes place (whatever the reasons) and not much intelligence or operational support is available. Therefore, the Army units start by putting in efforts to restore normalcy and not to "prevent" or "pre-empt". The job is, therefore, much more complex. Before, going any further we need to acknowledge that the Army is required to be called in when there is a failure of the administration; difficult to acknowledge but true.

Special Circumstances. The circumstances when the Army is called in, are nowhere near normal, therefore, it would be absurd to expect everything to function normally. Special laws are essential both for separating as also to protect individuals against long drawn legal battles for actions taken in good faith to restore normalcy. To people who cry hoarse "down with draconian laws"—I say special conditions need special laws. Also, it can be safely assumed that no relations of these "noise makers" have been kidnapped or killed or recruited against their will otherwise their tune would be quite different.

Support from Administration. Due to constraints of their own and perhaps due to lack of manifestation of firm political will; fairly frequently it is felt that support could be more. Add to this, problems like all weapons of a police post being lost without a shot being fired or an Armed Police person walking across to an insurgent group with his weapon (they offer good money and a so called post) and so on, the situation only gets grimmer. Accomodation, transport, telephone, etc. are also not so easily forthcoming. And the last straw (to cut a long story short) is when arrested militants (declared "black" and apprehended with weapons) are out of custody in less than three months time to thumb their noses at the Army.

How does the Army Function. A bit of insight into our structure, ethos and culture is essential to understand the Army's approach to combating insurgency. Also it is important, nay critical, to comprehend and appreciate how the Indian Army differs from all other armies of the world.

Insular Nature. The insular nature of the Army disallows intimate interaction and also disallows biases. A lot about the Army remains unknown to the public at large. We need to make people more aware. Our structure being what it is (people are drawn from the same village or even families) there is always a per group working. Another concept that is quite unknown to people is "religion of the troops is the religion of the officers"—when I commanded a Muslim company I always went to the Mosque: if I were to command a Sikh company I would go to the Gurudwara and so on.

Fight Militancy not Militants. The Army in its operations aims at fighting and neutralising militancy and not militants. The malaise has to be fought—the insurgents are only a manifestation. The Army never refer to the insurgents as enemy because they, possibly more than anyone else understand how diverse we Indians are. Once an insurgent gives up violence it means he is just another citizen.

Note: Our record of following our ethos, even when dealing with Prisoners of War is enviable because we are termed "gentleman's army".

No Policy of Elimination. Unlike other counter insurgency operations of the world (Philippines, Indonesia, Vietnam, Algeria, erstwhile Malaya, even erstwhile East Pakistan) the Indian Army does not follow a policy of "elimination" of militants. This continues despite grave provocation but this is followed because we are quite clear that the insurgent is not an enemy. A comparative study of casualty and apprehensive figures will indicate this quite easily. This policy will have to be continued because this is what makes us credible (irrespective of who writes what).

Intelligence Network. The Police should have covered this area (intelligence) because it is their strength (due to permanency and nature of work) but it is found that the Army has to rely on its own innovativeness.

Nature of Preparedness: Since the Army has to be constantly prepared for all its roles, turnovers are essential and one cannot be deployed in a particular area for very long. This has its connected consequences.

Specific Searches. The days of typical cordon and searches are over. Now very small and specific areas need attention at a time thereby reducing the hardship of the general populace. The Army understands lack of co-operation by the local population, mainly due to fear of reprisals. Unlike other counter insurgency operations of the world there are no penal taxes laid or mass punishments meted out. Unfortunately, people don't seem to appreciate this and, in fact, take advantage of it (with cues from militants) to lodge false FIRs etc.

Strengths of the Army. Stability and impartiality of the Army have always been constant. Also concern for resolving the militancy has always been genuine. Discipline, the cornerstone of the Indian Army is our greatest strength. If and when aberrations do occur (quite likely when such large numbers are deployed in the circumstances already described) the punishments in the Army are so intense that a man from the civil street can never imagine it. For an offence, when a person from the public would get three months in jail, the Armyman would get possibly a seven years in jail and would, of course, be dismissed from service. Very harsh but deterrent punishments are essential in the Army.

Minimum force. The Army does not use all the force available to it; never uses major area weapons. Only the bare essential force is brought to bear.

Media

An objective (utopian?) media coverage would assist greatly in resolving insurgency, but 'scoops' are so important that visits to hideouts, which give further fillip to insurgents, become the lifeline. STD facilities have made it possible for easy reporting—never mind the truth. Egos run so high that media persons do not like to correct themselves. But, to be fair to media persons the Army is not very forthcoming in providing information either. We, in the Army, have not fully absorbed the importance of *"timeliness"* in reporting news. In a fast moving era news becomes history very soon; and history is of no use to the reporters who deal with "here and now". But that does not absolve the media person from being truthful. He/she needs to make all out efforts in this regard and must add on his/her own analysis regarding "possibility" and "probability" of the news being reported. The Army, on its part, must understand the threat (from militants) under which people function, specially the regional press. They know the militants will kill them and they know the Army won't—so a balanced treatment is needed. Being in operations is essential for media persons to understand the pressures.

Human Rights

Fashionable as it has become we cannot but talk about it, it would take long to join issues on this topic so I will just put across a few points for consideration.

- Human rights violations cannot apply only to the Army.
- Some media people say "it is the job of the Armyman to die—he is paid for it".
- When bullets are flying where are these activists?
- When people are shot in *mandirs* where are they?
- It is easy to talk against the Army because they know that response will not be physical.
- They pass judgment without experience or exposure: theory is very different from ground reality.
- Human rights (specially to live) are upheld most by the Army be it in earthquakes, floods, train accidents or in use of minimum force.
- Are all human rights organisations self-sufficient? Or are some dependent on foreign grants?
- Countries who make the maximum noise on human rights need to first stand trial for the rape and massacre of the Red Indians, for Hiroshima and Nagasaki, for Vietnam, for Jallianwala Bagh and Indigo plantations, for the concentration camps for the "comfort" workers—*et al.*

If anything, the Army upholds human rights in the most exemplary fashion. Aberrations, if any are quickly and very strictly dealt with.

Conclusion

Love for the country and loyalty towards it cannot be the sole prerogative of the Army. If one wishes to enjoy freedom one has to work for it. Awareness has to be increased specially among students (our future) and armchair critics and decision-makers (and there's no dearth of them). Right to protest is well accepted but the right of any motley group to usurp authority must be put down severely. Any failure (or omissions) on the part of the police and administration also needs to be harshly dealt with. Compromise and complacency cannot be a way of life.

Some recent incidents (Sanjoy Ghose, Brigadier Vishakan) almost point to militants becoming "contract killers" for a price. This needs to be monitored and analysed.

Savagery and civilisation have to be looked into, to place ourselves somewhere on the continuum. In many other countries the policy followed against militants is "bury them or buy them". These constitute points to ponder. In all fairness, as per those countries, a confirmed militant had no "rights"—his house was taken over, his family was uprooted (sometimes kept in custody as counter threat). Thank heavens our country continues to be civilised in this respect.

Selfish interests seem to be now ruling insurgent's policies—Majuli is a prime example; as are attacks on trains. It is important to analyse who benefits from continuing insurgency. Obviously, if people sometimes wonder "would success really be welcomed by all?"—there is a need to dig a little more.

5

State Atrocities as History

Counter Insurgency Operations and Human Rights Violations in North East India

Sajal Nag

Acts and events of State violence, genocide, army atrocities, police brutality, minority persecution etc., have long remained outside the domain of historiography. Reporting such happenings of human right violations are still considered jobs of activists and voluntary organisations for generating nationalist sentiments (*e.g.* Blackhole tragedy or Jalianwala Bagh tragedy in Indian historiography as 'events' historical enough to attract/deserve historical research.

The Naga, Mizo and Methei resistance of the haegemony of the Indian State over them are as old as Indian independence The Indian State condemned such resistance as 'Secessionism' and 'Insurgency' and launched counter-insurgency operations of various denominations, though people outside the North East India had very little information about the nature and consequences of these operations or the regular perpetration of human rights violations in the area. Few reports in radical journals and reports by activists like Nandita Haksar and Luithui are all that we have. But as time moved on, these acts of inhumanity have become an inextricable part of Naga, Mizo or Methei history.

The Army atrocities which include murder, rape, torture, destruction and displacement are not mere punitive retaliations but are meant to be display of might and power of the State. It is aimed at terrorising the entire community, traumatise and outrage them to such an extent that the community is emotionally paralysed, physically inebilitated and intellectually demoralised for any revolutionary ideology to ever appeal to them again; they become subservient to the State ruling over them.

In the following pages we relate instances of human rights violations in the Naga, Mizo and Methei regions of NE India.

Negotiating Resistance

The Nehru Government of free India had not foreseen the snowballing of secessionist movements in the post-colonial India. By 1950, the Indian nation seemed to have consolidated itself except for the case of Kashmir and the Nagas. The tininess of the Naga Population *vis-a-vis* its size and might, had made the Indian State complacent about the eventual Naga acceptance of Indian suzerainty.[1] Nehru knew that the Nagas were a tough people and was, therefore, against any hasty attempt to absorb them.[2] He felt that if the Government keeps its head cool and restrains its hand the whole movement may gradually fizzle out, because it leads to nothing.[3] But the unfortunate event of March 1953 at Kohima when Nagas walked out of the meeting Nehru was to address, deteriorated the situation. Nehru blamed the Assam Chief Minister Bishnuram Medhi for the mishandling, who in turn sacked the Deputy Commissioner.[4] Nehru even put it on record that the Naga situation worsened due to its mishandling by certain officials.[5] To avenge the misconduct the Assam Government cracked down on the Naga National Council (NNC) activists. The NNC office and the NNC scretary, T. Sakhrie's place was raided. *Naga Nation*, the NNC mouthpiece was banned. Following the declaration of Tuensang area as free, bitter factional fight amongst the Nagas and the Indian army moved into the Naga hills. On 31 January the entire Naga hills was declared Disturbed Area by the promulgation of the Naga Hills Disturbed Area Ordinance and Assam Maintenance of Public Order of 1953. The Assam Police was replaced by the Indian army. The Armed Forces Special Power Act was promulgated for added power to the army. As secessionism did not peter out and military operations too did not bear substantial fruits, more power was given to the army authorities under the Nagaland Security Regulation Act of 1962 and North East Armed Force Special Power Act 1972. The Armed Forces (Special Power) Act of 1958 as amended by the Armed Forces (Assam and Manipur), Special Power (Amendment) Act of 1972 was enforced in the area. Similarly, the MNF in Mizoram was declared unlawful in the wake of its attempted coup in March 1966. The Extraordinary Gazette Notification of the Government of India published in March 6, 1966 cited that the MNF activities were "prejudicial to the security of the Mizo district in the State of Assam and the adjoining parts of the territory of India." The

Central Government by effecting necessary amendment ordered that Rule 32 of the Defence of India Rules 1962 shall be applicable to the MNF. Simultaneously various other orders similar to that of Naga hills were passed to provide additional power to the armed forces which will be discussed below. The Disturbed Area Act was extended over Manipur on 21 July 1976 and the Armed Forces Special Power Act 1958 was also imposed. Although the Government was forced to withdraw the Act on August 1, 1978 it was reimposed on 8 September 1980. The Army was called in to deal with the insurgency. A separate 'M' (Mike) sector was opened specifically to counter the Methei insurgents. Since then Manipur had virtually been under the army rule.

Although the Indian State did not formulate any conscious anti-insurgency policy, its method of dealing with insurgency situation developed a pattern over time. It preferred to ignore the secessionist movements at the initial period when such movement were weak. But should it develop significant strength it would be declared illegitimate and force would be resorted to crush it. Simultaneous efforts would also be made to win over the moderate section of the secessionists through conciliation and thereby alienate the extremist elements. The emphasis would be to get the secessionist movement peter out on its own. But even after army operations, if it continued to pose problems to the polity, accords were to be entered into with the leaders of the movement whereby major implementable demands of the insurgents would be granted while the secessionists would be expected to give up their claims to sovereignty.

The Stick : Enter the Army

While moving the army into the Naga hills, Prime Minister Nehru's reported instructions to the Chief of the Army staff was to deal with the Nagas as 'fellow Indians" and use "moderate force". Following this, the Order issued by the Chief of the Army Staff to the armed forces was in the same spirit:

> You must remember that all the people of the area in which you are operating are fellow Indians. They may have a different religion, may pursue a different way of life but they are Indians and the very fact that they are different yet form a part of India, is a reflection of India's greatness. Some of these people are misguided and have taken to arms against their people and are disrupting the peace of the area. You are to protect the mass of the people from these disruptive elements. You are not here to fight the people in the area but to protect them. You are fighting

only those who threaten the people and who are a danger to the lives and properties of the people. You must therefore, do everything possible to win their confidence and respect and help them feel that they belong to India.[6]

But when the Movement took the form of organised insurgency, the Government of India concluded that they had no option but to deal with it for all practical purposes as purely military solution though it was never officially acknowledged as such.[7] Nehru was successful in vetoing the suggestion for machine gunning from the air.[8] The failure of the army to effectively deal with the Naga Movement also did not harden Nehru. "It must always be remembered that if the Nagas are made to feel that they have no alternative but to fight and die, they will prefer doing so."[9] So Nehru urged the army to act swiftly but not brutally. Thimayya, the most distinguished of the senior army commanders was ordered to take charge immediately. But Nehru's objective of wining the minds and hearts of people without terrifying or frightening them did not succeed. It ended up doing what it did not intend to do. The army, frustrated by failures to tackle the insurgency did not act with restrain. Enormous power was given to the army vide various Acts during the successive governments, specially during the Prime Ministership of Mrs. Indira Gandhi. For example, under Section 4 of the Armed Forces Special Power Act (as amended, 1972) any commissioned officer, warrant officer, non-commissioned officer or any other person of equivalent rank in the armed forces may use force in a disturbed area:

(a) if he is of opinion that it is necessary to do so for the maintenance of public order, after giving such due warning as he may consider necessary, fire upon or otherwise use force, even to the causing of death, against any person who is acting in contravention of any law or order for the time being in force in the disturbed area prohibiting the assembly of five or more persons or the carrying of weapons or of things capable of being used as weapons or of fire-arms, ammunition or explosive substances;
(b) ...Destroy any arms dump, prepared or fortified position or shelter from which armed attacks are made or are likely to be made or are attempted to be made, or any structure used as a training camp for armed volunteers or utilised as a hide-out by armed gangs or absconders wanted for any offence;
(c) arrest without warrant, any person who has committed a congnisable offence or against whom a reasonable suspicion exists that he has committed or is about to commit a congnisable offence and may use such force as may be necessary to effect the arrest;

(d) enter and search without warrant any premises to make any such arrest as aforesaid or to recover any person believed to be wrongly restrained or confined or any property reasonably suspected to be stolen property or any arms, ammunition or explosive substance believed to be unlawfully kept in such premises, and may for that purpose use such forces as may be necessary.[10]

As can be seen, the laws on surveillance were so carefully phrased that no offence needed to be committed, nor even contemplated by the tribals to enable any havilder of the Indian army to take drastic actions against the former. The Nagaland Security Regulation of 1962 conferred special provisions for search, giving the same latitude to the police officer to determine intent. The police had a right to search "any street, alley, public place or open space" to check whether a person is carrying "in contravention of the law" not only corrosive substances or explosives "but any article which (the police) have reason to believe is being or is about to be used in contravening any order.[11] Although there were no references to any power to the army to burn down civil habitation, villages and granaries were systematically burnt down by taking shelter under the provisions mentioned in (b) above. Section 5 of the Armed Forces special Power Act 1958 also stipulated that " any person arrested and taken into custody under this regulation shall be made over to the officer-in-charge of the nearest police station with the least possible delay together with a report of the circumstances occasioning the arrest." But taking advantage of the ambiguous phrase "least possible delay" the army would deal with the suspect themselves sometimes leading to his death without handing him over to the local police. The Government also armed itself with the right to obtain information. It could by an order ask any person to produce any such information or article in his possession. It was also empowered to impose collective punishment—not for commission of offences that may be held to be congnisable but for failing to fulfill responsibilities that the Government had demanded from the tribals. Section 7 of the Assam Maintenance of Public Order Act stated that "if it appears to the State that the inhabitants in any area are concerned in or abetting the commission of offences pre-judically affecting the public safety or the maintenance of supplies or services necessary to the life of the community or are harbouring persons concerned in the commission of such offences, are failing to render all assistance in their power to discover or to apprehend the offender or are suppressing material evidence, that State Government may impose a collective fine".

As against these, Section 6 of the Armed Forces Special Power Act 1958 (Amended in 1972) assured for good measure complete autonomy and immunity to the members of the armed forces personnel engaged in all such operations from being called upon to account for their actions:

> No prosecution, suit or other legal proceedings shall be instituted, except with the previous sanction of the Central Government, against any person in respect of anything done or purported to be done in exercise of powers conferred by regulation.[12]

While the armed forces personnel were thus given a free hand without any accountability, the tribals were not provided any legal redress. Section 34(1) of the Nagaland Security Regulations stipulated that "no court shall take cognisance of the provisions of this regulation or of any order made thereunder, except on a report in writing of the facts constituting such contravention made by a public servant." The tribals, therefore, could not seek redress from courts against all the arbitrary powers that the State had over him—requisition of his property, destruction of his food stock, burning of his habitation, removing him without so much as a right to raise a slogan against the State, deprivation of his access to his forest resources without providing him with any alternative for his subsistence.

Having thus been armed with such absolute powers the Indian army set out to crush the rebellions in the respective states of Nagaland, Mizoram and Manipur. Reporting the uprising in Mizo hills which necessitated the deployment of the army, Gulzari Lal Nanda, the then Minister of Home Affairs said to the Parliament on March 3, 1966:

> We have been in touch with the Government of Assam in regard to certain serious incidents that have occurred in the night of February 28, March 1, in the Mizo Hills district. The position as ascertained from the State Government, is that between 10.30 p.m. on the 28th February and 3 a.m. on the 1st March, some tribals resorted to acts of lawlessness and violence at Lunglei, Aizwal, Eayrangte (Vairengte), Chawngte, and Chinluang (Chhimluang) in their attempt to disrupt communications and overawe public servants. The total number who took part in all these places is about eight hundred to one thousand three hundred. There are reasonable grounds to believe that these tribals are led by extremist elements in the Mizo National Front. The first attack was at about 10.30 p.m. on the 28th February on the sub-treasury at Lungleh. A gang of five hundred to one thousand strong attacked a camp of Security Forces and an Assam Rifles Post. This attack was beaten back and some of the attackers were stated

to have been killed. On our side, two men of the Assam Rifles were killed and three wounded. The whereabouts of the Sub-Divisional officer of Lunglei who was surrounded are still not known. The latest reports to reach from Lungleh indicate that some firing is going on at Lungleh. At about 2.00 a.m. on the 1st March a number of persons attacked the Telephone Exchange at Aizwal and an hour later the District Treasury was also attacked by about one hundred to one hundred fifty persons who took away ten rifles, two bayonets, some rounds of 303 ammunition and cash from the single lock of the Treasury. They tried to break open the double lock but they did not succeed. At about 1.30 a.m. on the 1st March, a gang of one hundred to one hundred and fifty people armed with *lathis* (clubs) surrounded the Sub-Divisional Officer, Public Works Department, at Eayrangte (Vairente) and asked him to get out of the district. The mob took the key from *Chowkidar* (caretaker) and took over the departmental stores and the jeep. There were similar encounters at Coinluang and Chawngte at which a number of persons belonging to the Mizo National Front were killed. No fresh incidents have been reported from the morning of the 1st March but delayed reports of the rebels seizing two police stations on the 1st have been received. While full details of all these incidents are yet to be gathered. I learn from the Chief Minister that the situation at Aizwal is now fully under control. The Commissioner of Silchar Division, the Inspector General of the Assam Rifles and a senior Army Officer have visited Aizwal and made an on the spot assessment of the situation.[13]

The Minister of Home Affairs continued his report as follows:

As a result of this, the Army has been asked to deal with the situation in Mizo Hill District. Transport of troops to Aizwal by helicopter has been going on this morning and troops are also moving by road to Aizwal and are expected to reach there by noon today. The armed police forces have been placed under the operational control of the Army for dealing with the disturbances. The army will be in charge of the operation for as long as necessary in support of the civil administration. Curfew has been imposed, an intensive patrolling has been started. The State Government issued a notification declaring Mizo Hill District Area under the Armed Forces (Assam and Manipur) Disturbed Area Act and under the Assam Disturbed Areas Act. This confers special powers on the Armed Forces and the State police. The report that a pirate radio is functioning inciting the Mizo tribals to declare independence and resort to lawlessness is being checked up. The Director General, All India Radio is arranging to monitor the transmission of any of the pirate radio and steps are being taken to find out the location of the transmitter if in fact it exists. There is enough evidence to come to the conclusion that these acts are part of a campaign by misguided extremist elements in the Mizo National Front to back their demand for independence. Governments are determined to put down the disturbances with utmost firmness and speed, and to restore peace and order. They are confident this will be achieved within a short period.[14]

Immediately on receipt of information about the outbreak of violence in Mizoram, the Government sent a team of officers, consisting of the Commissioner of the Division, the I.G.P. (Assam Rifles) and a senior officer of the Army to Aizwal to study the situation on the spot and suggest ways and means to quell the rebellion. It suggested that the situation should be handed over to the army. On March 2, 1966, the Government of Assam declared the district as a disturbed area. The army reached Aizwal on the evening of 6th March. The security forces gained complete control of the district headquarters, after which the army marched towards Lunglei but the town was completely under the control of the rebels. The army threatened to bomb it. The church leaders interfered and requested the army not to bomb the town and that they would secure its surrender. The troops entered Lunglei on 13th March, Champai on the next day and Demagri on March 17. All the important towns and posts were cleared of the influence of the volunteers of the MNF. The MNF volunteers took to the jungles, Pakistan and Burma.

On the March 6, 1966, the MNF was declared unlawful. The State Government dropped one lakh leaflets in the district by air to inform the people of the facts of the situation and warn them not to participate in any unlawful activities. The army took over and launched the counter-insurgency operation. The counter-insurgency combing operation of the Indian army also followed a set pattern in all the three areas under discussion. On the strength of a tip off from the State intelligence official or local informers a particular village or a locality, where the insurgents had reportedly taken shelter would be marked. Curfew would be imposed on the area all of a sudden in the early morning hours when everybody was asleep and no one could run away. The area then was cordoned off and announcements were made over loudspeakers that curfew had been imposed and no one should venture out of their houses. Operation was then launched with children, women and old people screened and frisked inside the houses and rest taken out in the open field where tents had already been built for interrogation through an identifier.[15] Occasionally encounters broke out between the insurgents and the army during such operations resulting in casualties.

Grouping of Villages

The Indian State took its lessons in anti-insurgency measures from the British and the Americans in Malaya and Vietnam respectively. In fighting the Malayan Races Liberation Army in Malaya the British General Briggs had mooted what was known as Operation Starvation.[16] Its object was to deprive the guerillas of its source of food and stop them from taking shelter in the villages. Besides imposing restriction on the selling and distribution of food items, the army also rearranged the Chinese settlements and regrouped the tin and mine workers so as to check the infiltration and exfiltration of the guerillas with the settled population. The population was no longer scattered. It was concentrated in units of 40,000 that moved into just 400 villages, which made it easy to keep strict watch over them.[17] The device was later tested by the Americans in Vietnam. Field Marshall Maneckshaw advocated the application of the same in the insurgency affected areas of Nagaland and Mizoram[18], where army did not have much success allegedly due to the co-operation of the villagers with the insurgents. Tarlok Singh, Member of the Planning Commission visited Mizoram in 1966 and approved the regrouping of villages euphemistically called economically viable village.[19] Replicating the British and American army in Malaya and Vietnam respectively, the Indian army would move and surround the notified villages before dawn, issue quick notice to the villagers to take their bedding etc. and move to the new site where they were issued identity cards and barricades were constructed to prevent mobility. The old and abandoned villages with their granaries were then burnt. About fifty to hundred villages were initially shifted from their original sites and settled along the highway and placed under the charge of the army men so that these villages were isolated from the insurgents and a strict vigil could be maintained. Although the regrouping facilitated army operation it caused acute human trauma to the villagers. "In many instances villagers were forced to move out of their old dwellings at gun-point because they were reluctant to leave what had been their home for generations. In most cases the villagers had to leave on a day's notice. There was no time to pack their belongings and it was not possible to carry everything at one time. Animals had to be killed and food grains had to be hidden in the forest. If there was no time to hide food-grains they were burnt with the houses. As soon as the people left the place, the army personnel ransacked the houses, keep the valuables for themselves and then burnt them down.

Hidden food-grains in the forest when discovered were taken away by the troops and hoarded or villagers were ordered to burn them."[20] The regrouping not only drastically altered the settlement pattern of the Mizos, it had a substantial impact on their socio-economic and cultural life. Before the introduction of the scheme, there were 764 villages distributed in three sub-divisions of Aizwal, Lunglei and Chhimtuipi excluding the two towns of Aizwal and Lunglei. Of these 764 villages 516 were evaluated and grouped into 110 grouping centres while 138 villages were excluded from the grouping scheme.[21] Thus after the completion of the grouping of villages in 1970, the number of villages in the districts was reduced from 764 to 248. In the Aizwal sub-division alone 456 villages before 1967 had been reduced to 112 villages involving population of 1,88,923 or approximately 95% of the rural population. One set of grouping took place along the Silchar-Aizwal-Lunglei-Champai highway and another along the secondary Lunglei-Lawagtai-Selling-Champai, Darhgawn-Bungzung-Khawbung-North Vanlaiphai-Serchip Road. The grouping was done under four distinct categories: Protected and Progressive Villages, New Grouping centres, Voluntary Grouping Centres and Extended Loop Areas. Although the claim by the Indian government was that the grouping was necessary for the economic development of these distant villages, the operation was carried out under the Defence of India Rules 1962 and Assam Maintenance of Public Order Act 1953.

Such forcible resettlement shattered the foundation of the economic and social structure of Mizos. Except the areas where wet rice cultivation was practised (Bilkhawtlir, Champai, Thenzawl) *Jhum* cultivation experienced total dislocation[22] because

1. area of cultivable land had been drastically reduced as the ratio of people to land had been forcibly increased and the curfew compelled the villagers to cultivate only in those areas which was within half-a-days reach, so that they could go to the field and come back home before the curfew hours.
2. *Jhum* cultivation, the basic method of agriculture of the tribals became virtually impossible as *Jhum* went only with scattered habitation. To exacerbate the situation further the tribal institution of *tlawbawk*, hut built near the *Jhum* for camping during harvesting and weeding, was abolished. Thus, villagers had to waste precious time in travelling to the fields and returning home for mid-day meals.

3. Harrassment in the initial checking of identity cards and periodic curfew for collective interrogation or for re-checking identity cards further reduced working hours on the fields.
4. Male labourers on whom agriculture in Mizoram depended heavily were rounded up and sent off to work on border roads in Kashmir or were forced to act as porters for the troops during its movement.
5. Access to the forest beyond the prescribed limits for vital additional food gathering was denied to the tribals by the army.
6. Since possession of even small arms was prohibited, hunting, the only alternative during famines, also became impossible. As a cumulative result there was a drastic fall in agricultural production and acute food shortage. Famine-like conditions were experienced throughout 1968, 1969 and 1970. Landlessness emerged as a new phenomenon. In a resettled area where 400 families were grouped, 90% did not have any land. As a result, the villagers became wholly dependent on the rations supplied by the Government which was denied to them at will causing immense suffering. Soon, there was a large scale migratory movement towards the towns of Aizwal and Lunglei where educated but pauperized people began to crowd around the white collar employment sector.

Violation of Human Rights

Although the Prime Minister and the Chief of the Army staff claimed that the "army had shown remarkable patience in the face of considerable provocations" the Human Rights bodies reported widespread abuse of human rights in Mizoram, Nagaland and Manipur. As early as 1956 the Army killed a veteran Naga physician Dr. Haralu which sent shock waves through out the Naga hills. Prime Minister Nehru himself admitted the death of Dr. Haralu during one of the army operations and described it as one of the most regrettable mistakes.[23] Armed repression was gradually mounted. "There was heavy deployment in the Tuensang area. Following report of army activities, Gavin Young of the *London Observer* visited Naga hills during February 20 to March 10, 1960, who subsequently published his report in the form of a book entitled *The Nagas, An Unknown War—India's Threat to Peace.* Following reports of several such incidents the Naga Peoples' Movement for Human Rights was formed to campaign against the army excesses in Naga hills. In Mizo hills disturbed by the army atrocities,

Brigadier Sailo an ex-armyman himself formed Human Rights Committee. In 1974 two public leaders from NE India, G. G. Swell (MP) and J.J. M. Nicolas Roy (MLA) prepared one such report and submitted to the Indian Parliament.[24] According to these reports the forms of repression used by the military and paramilitary forces were execution in public, mass rape, deforming of sex organs, mutilating limbs and body, electric shock, puncturing of eyes, hanging people upside down, putting people in smoke filled rooms, burning down of houses, food-stocks and crops, concentration camps, suffocating a person by fully covering with a dripping wet blanket, economic blockade leading to starvation and forced labour[25], the last was practised widely by the British in Naga hills when they were fighting to subdue the Nagas. Women were specially singled out for committing indignities like rape, parading nude in the open and assault on pregnant women. The Human Rights Committee set up by Brig. T. Sailo collected detailed evidence on thirty six cases of army arocities ranging from rape and torture to collective execution listing the names and ranks of the army officers involved. The most shocking incident being the mass rape at Kolashib (1966):

> In Kolashib, 50 miles of Aizwal, the army rounded up all the menfolk of the village, about 500 of them. They were collected, made to lie down on the ground on their stomachs and then were kicked, beaten, trampled upon and confined for the night. At night groups of soldiers moved about the village. They broke into the houses, helped themselves with everything of value—clocks, sewing machines, clothes etc... and raped the women.[26]

Another incident in the same village at the same time as recorded was:

> There was the case of a woman in an advanced stage of pregnancy—Lalthumai, wife of a cultivator, Lalkhangliana. Five soldiers appeared in her house one night, took the husband out of the house at gun-point and then while two soldiers held the woman down, the third committed rape.[27]

Sailo's report created a furore in the Indian Parliament.[28] The pattern was all too similar also in Naga hills. Amnesty International, which also compiled a report on this, recorded cases of sexual abasement by the Assam Rifles personnel whose names were known to the Amnesty International[29]. At least three women complained of having been raped by commanding officer. On January 24, 1986 Miss Luingmla was murdered by two army officers when she resisted rape. A belated general court martial was held on July 11, 1988 in which the main accused in the above case Lieutenant Mandhir Singh was sentenced to life imprisonment and cashiering for murder.[30] However, the army threatened and harassed the social workers who protested against this crime by taking recourse to the provisions of the Armed Forces Special Power Act to deny jurisdiction of the Chief Judicial Magistrate Court which had taken cognisance of the crime (May 16, 1986). A horrifying incident took place at Oinam on July 9, 1987. Fifteen men were tortured to death by the Assam Riffles, another six died of continuous torture like starvation and standing in the open on one leg for the whole day. Six babies also died of starvation and lack of medical facilities.[31] Two pregnant women were forced to deliver their babies in full view of the jawans. About 125 houses were burnt down or dismantled, valuables taken away and *Jhum* crops destroyed. On receiving complaint from some social workers the Gauhati High Court directed the Session Court at Imphal to record first hand evidence from the villagers about the alleged offences by the Assam Rifles jawans. The Naga Peoples Movement of Human Rights moved a *habeas corpus* petition on behalf of the two women whose husbands were taken away by the 21 Sikh Regiment never to return[32],— a pastor and a school teacher. These two were reportedly not connected in any way with the insurgent activities. In a historic judgment in the *Sebastian Hongray versus Union of India* case (AIR, 1984, SC 1626) the Supreme Court of India directed the army to pay one Lakh rupees damage to each of the widows and directed the District Superintendent of Police to begin prosecuting the guilty army men. The Kohima Baptist Women's Union submitted a memorandum to the Prime Minister of India reporting such atrocities because "reports of such incidents that occur in our state" were "not heard by you" and "our moans and wails are muffled and lost in the deep gorges of thickly forested mountains in this part of the country."[33]

> We do not believe that the army officers were directed by the Government of India to act so. They seem to be here with the high and mighty attitude of the ancient barbarian conquerors. We pray that misdeed of a small section of the security forces must not be allowed to undermine the very basis of decent human existence and bring disrepute to the good name of the Indian army.[34]

The incident referred to here took place on July 11, 1971 when a strong column of the Maratha Regiment came to Yankeli, a village in Wokha sub-division of Mokikchong district of Nagaland, at about 6 pm. They herded all the womenfolk in a house. Then the Captain "handpicked" four girls from among the crowd who were taken to the church building. One Mr. Peleo was also taken along with the girls. Once inside the church, Peleo was sent back and a 17 year old girls named Shachano was striped naked, her hands and legs were tied against the chair and after a brief interrogation she was taken to the pulpit and was raped by a Captain and second Lieutenant by turns. She was then led out, allowed to dress and sent away. The same was repeated with Mseno (15), Sukrumo (12) and Thungteno (11). In August 1977 Rano Baiza, MP from Nagaland narrated to a shocked audience at a Convention of Political Prisoners at New Delhi citing instances of human rights violation in the Naga hills.[35] In Matikhru village of Phek district the Indian army rounded up all the menfolk, executed them, hounded the women out and then razed the village down. Six Naga students of the Pfutsero Government School were kidnapped by the Indian army and later reportedly butchered. In Ignasumi village a pregnant woman was shot at while harvesting in the field and her dead body was dragged along the jungle route. When the villagers went to retrieve her battered body, they found it with the protruding head and limbs of the aborted baby. On July 11, 1977 the pregnant wife of a pastor was stoned and kicked so badly that the woman subsequently (30 July) aborted and a dead child with broken skull came out of her womb. On March 4, 1977 a young girl was raped in Nagaprum village of Ukhrul district of Manipur by Major Pundir and Captain Negy of the 95 Border Security Force. The girl who was raped in front of the villagers subsequently committed suicide.

Army fury would be worse if the insurgents had killed any of the Army personnel in an ambush. The army would in such case retaliate with an angry attack on the villagers to avenge the murder of their colleagues. When in one such ambush 22 Army jawans were killed by the NSCN on February 19, 1982 the retaliation was on the villages of Ukhrul, the base of the NSCN. The villagers suffered untold atrocities at the hands of the rampaging armymen.[36] At the Convention on Political Prisoner, the Naga Human Rights activist L. Luithui conveyed to the Indian people that "the only freedom the Nagas know is the freedom to obey and submit to the military authorities... But none of us love this freedom. We hate it bitterly because this freedom ironically means the freedom to be insulted, tortured, raped and executed in public. In deep agony we wonder how all these things are going on in our land without any protest from the great Indian people..."[37]

The Army atrocities and the trauma caused to the people by the counter-insurgency measures have since become a part of the tribal folklores. There is a Naga folk song about an Angami girl who was raped by a member of the Indian Army which goes:

> She was a happy child
> She went out to the rice fields
> Singing like a free bird.
> She was born of the rugged mountain.
> But one day a soldier came to her land
> She was tortured and raped
> He took her dignity away,
> Her home is where she belongs
> And she will rise up again to
> Sing in glory and
> Tell her people a new story.

The inhuman trauma caused to the tribals by regrouping were movingly captured in some of the Mizo folk songs composed by the village bard Suakliana of Sialsuk.[38]

> Pity of Pities, our villages are grouped
> Everywhere in Zoram, life has lost its beauty
> Women, children, men gathered from every hill
> Feel homeless and stranded like Riakmaw bird
> In the new place where friends and loved ones gathered
> I still pine for our old motherland (village)
> where the gentle prince (God) who loves us also dwells.

Or,

> I dare not contemplate this grief of our land
> Departed are our civilised white skinned mentors
> Oh God, who succor the poor, I pray thee
> Set our tottering land on its feet again.

Or,

> Silent are the country sides and the Churches where we
> Lived and sang with our near and dear ones,
> Lovely dones yearning for their mate haunt them now
> And frequented by flock of birds they now lie forlorn.

And lastly,

> O Lord forgive us all our sins and trespasses which
> Have caused us this uprootedness guide on,
> Holy Spirit, Zion's fair flowers
> Hold me with your powerful and that bless men
> Till I reach your sweet and bright heavenly home.

NOTES AND REFERENCES

1. It was only after the secessionist threats from the Tamils, Kashmiris during the dangerous decade of the 60s that constitutional safeguards were evolved against secessionism. The Indian Constitution was amended (sixteenth) which sought to prevent fissiparous trends engendered by regional and linguistic loyalties and preserve territoral integrity of the country.

   Amending Article 19 (refering to the freedom of speech) it enabled the legislatures to penalise any individual who questioned the sovereignty and integrity of the country.
2. S. Gopal, *Jawaharlal Nehru: A Biography,* Vol. 2, Delhi, 1979, p. 207.
3. *Nehru to B. R. Medhi,*, 25 May 1951, cited in *ibid.*, p. 208.
4. Robert Trumbull, *As I see India*, New York, 1986, pp. 136-180.
5. Jawaharlal Nehru, *'A Note by the Prime Minister on his tour of the North Eastern Frontier Provinces',* Shillong, 1952.
6. Cited in V. Elwin, Nagaland, Shillong, 1961, pp. 60-61.
7. Statement made by the Prime Minister in the Parliament 23rd August 1956, Shillong, 1956, pp. 1-4.
8. Nehru to Defence Secretary, 19 June 1956, in S. Gopal *op. cit.*, p. 211.
9. Nehru to K. N. Katju, Defence Minister, 28 July 1956, in *ibid.*, p. 212.
10. Also cited in Amrita Rangasami, 'Mizoram: Tragedy of our Making", in *Economic and Political Weekly,* April 15, 1978, pp. 653-662, N. Haksar and M. Luithui, *Nagaland File*, New Delhi, 1984, pp. 176-186.
11. *Ibid.*
12. *Ibid.*
13. *Parliament Debates,* Vol. 55, No. 10-22, February 28 March 17, 1966 Rajya Sabha, Govt. of India, New Delhi, pp. 2125-2126
14. *Ibid.*, pp. 2126-2127
15. Sreekant Khandeka and Raghu Rai, "The Army Takes Charge", in *India Today,* December, 1-15, 1980, pp. 14-21 Parmila Dandavate *et al*, 'Report of a Fact Finding Team', in A. R. Desai (Ed) *Repression and Resistance in India,* Bombay, 1990, pp. 291-308.
16. Edgar O' Balance, "Malaysia: The Communist Insurgent War", cited in Amrita Rangasami, *op. cit.*
17. *Ibid.*
18. S. Chatterjee, *Mizoram Encyclopaedia,* Vol. 2, Jaico, Delhi, 1990 pp. 355-56.
19. *Ibid.*
20. Vumson, *Zo History,* Aizwal, n.d. pp. 284-285.
21. C. Nunthara, "Grouping of Villages in Mizoram: Its Social and Economic Impact", *Economic and Political Weekly,* July 25, 1981 pp. 1237-1240.

22. *Ibid.*, Amrita Rangasamy, *op. cit.* Chaitanya Kalbag, "The North East : The Human Tragedy (Mizoram Groups Therapy)" in *India Today*, October 31, 1982.
23. Nehru's speech in the Lok Sabha, August 23, 1956.
24. G.G. Swell and J.J. M. Nicholas Roy, *Suppression of Mizos in India: An Eye Witness Report.* This report was submitted to the Govt. of India, 1966. A smuggled copy of which was later published in Pakistan by Freoze Sons, Karachi, n.d.
25. Govinda Mukhoty, 'The Army Atrocities in Naga Areas : Peoples' Union for Democratic Rights", New Delhi. 1987.

    Amnesty International, "India: Operation Bluebird: A Case Study of Torture and Extra Judicial Execution in Manipur", NSA, 20/17/90, DISTR: SC/CO/GR, Glondon WX IX, BOJ, UK, 1990. M. Luithui and Nandita Haksar, *"Nagaland File : A Question of Human Rights,* Lancers, New Delhi, 1984 pp. 234-240." Report of NPMHR," in A.R. Desai (ed) *op. cit.*, pp. 291.
26. G. G. Swell-Nichols Roy, *op. cit.*, p. 5.
27. *Ibid.*, pp. 5-6.
28. Vumson, *op. cit.*, p. 29.
29. *op. cit.* see note 24.
30. Luithui and N. Hakasr, *op. cit.*
31. Amnesty International, *op. cit.*
32. Luithui and N. Hakasr, *op. cit,*
33. Memorandum to the Prime Minister, from Kohima Baptist Women's Union, Kohima, 22-08-1971.
34. *Ibid.*
35. Rano Saiza's speech cited in 'People for a New India', *Distrubed Areas: The Roots of Repression in Nagaland, Mizoram and Andhra Pradesh,* Bombay, 1979 p. 11.
36. Chaitanya Kalbagh, *op. cit.*
37. People for a New India, *Op. Cit.*, p. 16, A Report on the Army Atrocities was published in *India Today*. See Chaitanya Kalbag, *op. cit.*, International Work Group for Indigenous Affairs (IWGIA).

    The Naga Nation and Its Struggle Against *Genocide,* Copenhagen, 1986, pp. 135-229.
38. Cited in V. Venkata Rao, *et al, A Century of Government and Politics in North East India, (Vol. III,) Mizoram,* New Delhi, 1987, pp. 269-70.

6

Social Tension in North-East India

An Ecological Perspective

Abhik Gupta

At the international level, environmental issues, especially conflicting claims on control over raw materials, energy supplies, land, river basins, sea passages, etc., have often led to violent strife and conflict between countries. The attempt of Japan to gain control over oil, mineral and other resources in China and Southeast Asia during the Second World War, the armed intervention of American and allied forces during the invasion of Kuwait by Iraq to retain control over the vast oil resources in that region, and the extended conflict in the Western Sahara over rich phosphate deposits are well-known examples. Several researchers have suggested that environmental change, particularly those involving degradation and dwindling of natural resources would become an increasingly common cause of conflict in the coming years, especially if the world population keeps on increasing at the present rate.[1]

This paper attempts to show that the material basis for the social tension simmering in North-East India that has often led to violent conflicts between ethnic groups, and has culminated in armed insurgencies either directed against the State or against specific ethnic groups or both, lies in the competition over resources, in terms of agricultural and grazing land, forests, real estate in urban areas, jobs and the like. The historical process of settlement in NE India has followed a course where a large proportion of the above mentioned resources has remained with ethnic groups which are not original inhabitants of this region. In the early colonial and pre-independence times, when the population density in this region was low, the resources were proportionately plenty. However, the failure of the governments, both during the pre-and post-independence periods to adopt ecologically sustainable measures for conserving and augmenting the resource base in this region has led to a condition where different ethnic groups are competing fiercely for the limited, degraded and dwindling resources in the region. Even in those areas, where the feeling of deprivation and discontentment among the local inhabitants has not resulted in conflicts, a sense of unrest and tension clearly prevails in their minds. However, very often the apparent and immediate causes of conflicts have not been over resource-related issues, but totally different ones such as cultural 'swamping' by 'outsiders', linguistic and racial chauvinism, and even trifle events like soccer matches—one example being the Assamese-Bengali clashes over the Bordoloi Trophy Soccer Tournament results. One comes across similar situations in other countries also. Durham[2] traced the origin of the 1969 'Soccer War' between El Salvador and Honduras that was ignited over the outcome of a football match, to the migration of Upland El Salvadorean farmers to Honduras in search of more productive land, and their eventual expulsion from the latter country. Without trying to under-rate the importance of political and cultural factors, one may be permitted to say that resource limitations and the consequent competition over their control at least provided the nucleus around which the other factors accreted and often masked the former, eventually reaching a critical point of precipitation marked by agitations, conflicts and insurgency. The following sections of this article attempt to trace the ecological origins of social tension in two North-East Indian states, *viz.*, Assam and Meghalaya. As the process of resource exploitation and ecological degradation as well as the resultant communal fragmentation can be said to have begun with the British annexation of Assam in 1826, a historical evaluation of the patterns and processes of resource utilisation in the two states seems to be essential.

Colonisation of Land in Assam by Immigrants

The later part of Ahom rule in Assam (1769-1806) was marked by political chaos manifested in the form of a protracted civil war and a series of Burmese invasions (1817-24). The total population of Assam before the civil war was about 2.5 millions,[3] and this was reduced to about 1 million due to the ravages of civil war and invasions.[4] Although population size gradually increased after the civil war, population density in Assam remained fairly low in the late nineteenth and early twentieth centuries. In contrast, the North-eastern Bengal districts of

Mymensingh, Pabna, Bogra and Rangpur recorded high population densities during the same period (Table 1). This resulted in a scarcity of cultivable land in these districts. All the good quality land was already under rice cultivation, and any additional land available was brought under jute cultivation, which became an important commercial crop in North-eastern Bengal during the later half of 19th century. As Table 2 shows, more than 50 percent of the total land area in these districts was under cultivation by 1901. In contrast, barring Kamrup, the percentage of cultivated area to total area in the Brahmaputra Valley districts was less than 20 per cent, being as low as less than 10 per cent in Nowgong and Lakhimpur. It was, therefore, only natural that large numbers of cultivators from NE Bengal, especially Mymenshing, started migrating to occupy and cultivate first the *char* and other cultivable wastelands of Goalpara and subsequently of Nowgong, Darrang, parts of Kamrup and Lakhimpur. The Assam Census Report of 1931 took note of this and commented that the colonisation of Goalpara and Nowgong was complete, while the process was continuing in the Barpeta sub-division of Kamrup, and in Darrang and Lakhimpur districts as well. An estimated population of over half a million was thought to have transplanted itself from NE Bengal to Assam during 1901-1911. The South Salmara, Lakhimpur and Bilasipara police circles in Goalpara district recorded a population increase of 70.1, 61.8 and 88.6 per cents respectively during 1901-1911. In Barpeta sub-division of Kamrup, where settlers started coming in from around 1921, a decadal increase in population of 69 per cent was recorded during 1921-31.[5] Nevertheless, even in 1935-36 large portions of cultivable wastes were available for cultivation in Kamrup, Nowgong, Lakhimpur and Sibsagar districts (Table 3). In 1942, when the Saadulla Ministry was re-installed, the Land Development Scheme was revised, and grazing and forest reserve lands were opened to the immigrants. Each family was given 8 ha. of land and allowed to keep 5 heads of cattle. The immigrants, taking advantage of this, settled in large numbers in the forest areas. The number of such forest villages proliferated within no time, and more land was cleared, resulting in decimation and degradation of forests.

Another factor that contributed to the colonisation of land by immigrants was the setting up of tea plantations in Assam. The first experimental tea estate was established in Chabua, Dibrugarh district, in 1837. Subsequently, scores of tea estates sprung up in Brahmaputra and Surma Valleys during 1850-1900. As the indigenous people of these areas were not willing to work in the estates, the British started importing

Table 1: Density of Population per sq. mile in Brahmaputra Valley and North-Eastern Bengal in late 1800s-early 1900s

District	*1872*	*1881*	*1891*	*1901*	*1931*
Assam					
Kamrup	146	167	164	153	254
Darrang	69	80	90	99	206
Nowgong	68	82	90	68	144
Sibsagar	64	79	96	120	182
Lakhimpur	27	40	56	82	171
Goalpara	98	113	115	117	222
Bengal					
Mymensingh	377	483	548	618	823
Pabna	—	714	740	772	795
Bogra	—	505	562	629	785
Rangpur	—	600	591	617	242

Source : Nag (1990) and Pathak (1991).

Table 2: Status of Land in Assam and North-Eastern Bengal in 1901

District	*Area (Sq. miles)*	*Cultivated Area (Sq.Miles)*	*%of Cultivated Area to Total Area*
Assam			
Kamrup	3,858	798	20.7
Darrang	3,418	459	13.4
Nowgong	3,843	348	09.1
Sibsagar	4,996	804	16.1
Lakhimpur	4,529	388	08.6
Goalpara	3,961	670	16.9
Bengal			
Mymensingh	6,332	3,758	59.4
Pabna	1,839	1,231	66.9
Bogra	1,359	728	53.6
Rangpur	3,493	1,915	54.8

Source : Pathak (1991)

labours from provinces like Bihar, Bengal, Orissa, MP, UP and even Tamil Nadu, but chiefly from the Chhotanagpur region of Bihar. Taking advantage of the land-alienation and poverty in their native places, these labourers were lured to work for "lucrative" wages by agents called *Arkattis* to come to Assam. This process of recruitment began as early as in 1841, and by 1909, some 1,10,000 labourers were imported. This number swelled to 15,18,960 by 1936-37.[6] Furthermore, the time-expired labourers were settled on land near the tea estates to ensure that their services were available when any need arose. This practice of settlement of ex-tea labourers started as early as 1868 and by 1943-44, around 3,85,864 acres of land was brought under cultivation by these immigrants.

Table 3: Cultivable Wasteland available in Brahmaputra Valley (except Goalpara) in 1935-36

District	*Culturable Waste other than fallow (acres)*	*Net Area Sown (Acres)*	*%of Net Area Sown to Cultivable Area*	*Net Area Available (acres)*
Kamrup	4,18,050	98,326	23.5	3,19,724
Darrang	7,18,890	5,54,231	77.1	64,659
Nowgong	14,38,790	4,99,689	34.7	9,39,101
Sibsagar	14,82,573	2,54,856	17.2	12,27,717
Lakhimpur	14,86,599	5,03,442	33.9	98,157

Source : Kar (1990)

A third group of immigrants who occupied large chunks of land in Assam was the Nepalese. Since 1893-94 Nepalese graziers started occupying land in and near the unclassed forests of Assam and used them for grazing herds of buffalo and other livestock. These pastoralists occupied areas in Brahmaputra Valley, in the hill districts of Karbi Anglong and North Cachar, and in the *Bhoi* areas on the northern slopes of Khasi hills. They went for some cultivation, although they mainly depended on the production and sale of dairy products for their livelihood. By 1911-12, these herdsmen had some 86,389 buffaloes and 3,36,323 cows and bullocks.[7] As pressure on grazing land increased, more and more forest areas were affected by grazing.

Thus, British annexation of Assam transformed its demography, ecology and economy. The rapidly expanding tea industry took a severe toll on the forests. From a nominal 400 acres in 1859, some 3,83,821 acres of land were brought under tea in 1915. The *Char* lands on river Brahmaputra, the forested tracts, and the cultivable wastes were put under the plough, cultivation of cash crop like jute was encouraged. The total cropped area increased from 32,960 acres in 1881 to around 91,17,000 acres in 1947-48. It may be mentioned here that this area only marginally increased to about 93,82,387 acres in 1990-91,[8] indicating that the saturation point in land availability was probably attained as early as in 1947-48. The insignificant increase in the later years was most likely to have taken place through clearing of forests and/or reclamation of wetlands. The area under jute increased from less than 500 acres in 1901 to 58,000 acres in 1911.[9] But this economic 'upliftment' was achieved almost solely with the help of immigrant labour, cultivators and graziers. And in this was sown the seeds of future social tension and conflicts.

Ecological Factors Governing Immigration

An examination of the agrarian scenario in nineteenth century Assam may provide some clues to the unchecked colonization of land by outsiders, especially the cultivators from Eastern Bengal. During the Ahom period, and the decades following the British annexation of Assam in 1826, the agricultural technology in Assam was predominantly of primitive nature. While the Ahoms introduced wet rice cultivation in Upper Assam, shifting cultivation dominated the agricultural scene in the lower Assam districts of Kamrup and Nowgong.[10] The implements used, including the ploughshare, were very crude and simple, often made of roots of arecanut trees or bamboo, and the use of iron implements was limited.[11] Nevertheless, as the population size was very small, and the natural fertility of the soil high, the per capita production of paddy was on the average about 5 quintals per year. Thus, every district was self-sufficient in terms of paddy,[12] albeit at the subsistence level only. Most of the land was under paddy, followed by oilseeds like mustard. Cash crops such as sugarcane, cotton, tobacco and jute occupied an insignificant portion of the land under cultivation.[13] With the establishment and expansion of the tea industry, the existing level of food production was not sufficient to meet the demands of a rapidly increasing immigrant labour population. As the Assamese peasantry, with its primitive modes of agriculture, was unable to meet this demand, several British administrators advocated the settlement of farmers from Eastern Bengal, especially Mymensingh. Furthermore, it was also thought that the settlement of immigrant farmers from East Bengal on the cultivable wastes of Assam would provide relief from recurring famines and scarcity in the former. The Assamese middle class during the late nineteenth century also supported this view under the belief that only such a step could usher in economic progress in Assam.[14] Thus, the immigration of East Bengal farmers to Assam was a consequence of technological backwardness in agriculture that was manifested in the form of hoe cultivation of dry *Ahu* rice in the larger part of the Brahmaputra Valley, insignificance of cash crops, and the absence of a sizeable market sector for agricultural produces, including external trade.[15]

Ecological factors appear to have been the prime determinants of the readiness with which the East Bengal, especially the Mymensingh farmers, migrated to Assam, leaving their age-old homes and hearths for ever. The North-eastern Bengal districts of Rangpur, Pabna, Bogra and Mymensingh comprised an area especially suitable for multiple cropping and jute cultivation. The rich alluvial tracts in the catchment of the river Jamuna, through which the main stream of river Brahmaputra had flowed since the early 19th century, as well as that of the numerous other rivers in this region, therefore, attracted large numbers of farmers who settled on all available land. In Mymensingh, the cultivated area increased from 3,562 to 4,292 sq. miles during 1872-1910. More than 64 per cent of this expansion, equivalent to an area of 470 sq. miles, was in the infertile jungle tract of stiff clay in the Madhupur forest. This indicates that superior agricultural lands of the region could no longer support the burgeoning population, and by 1919 cultivation had 'almost reached its full limits' in Mymensingh.[16]

Furthermore, certain areas of Mymensingh, *viz.*, Netrakona and Kishoreganj sub-divisions, which contributed the most of immigrants, were underdeveloped, predominantly low-lying and prone to the vagaries of early floods and the spread of water hyacinth affecting the production of deep water paddy traditionally grown in these areas.[17] All these factors together contributed to the immigration of Mymensingh farmers during the first few decades of the 20th century. However, the land scarcity in East Bengal continued, and in 1938, 41.9% of agricultural families were found to hold 2 acres or less, and 20.6% between 2 and 4 acres of land, while around 5 acres were estimated to be required to maintain a family of five. In 1940, the holding size plunged further to slightly less than 1 acre for the majority of agricultural families. The migration, therefore, continued first to Goalpara, and then further upstream to Nowgong, Kamrup, Darrang and as far as Lakhimpur. As said earlier, this immigration was encouraged by the British in their colonial interests. Nevertheless, it was also a natural process in which overpopulation and consequent degradation of the natural resource base in the lower reaches of the Brahmaputra-Jamuna-Meghna catchment resulted in colonization of the upper reaches that lay in the State of Assam. Similar resource constraints in mountainous Nepal forced the Nepalese to fan out to Sikkim and Darjeeling and eventually to the foot hills of Assam including those of present day Meghalaya, in search of fresh grazing pastures.

Origins of Social Tension

The economic "upliftment" of Assam during the British rule was achieved almost solely with the help of immigrant labour. The benefits of this changed economy, however, did not reach the Assamese. Instead, more and more Assamese farmers became landless, often forced to sell their land to the immigrants, rural indebtedness increased manifold, and the indigenous cottage and handicraft industries like silk and handloom became nearly extinct. As almost all spare agricultural and grazing land were occupied by the immigrants, there was no scope for further agricultural expansion by the indigenous people. The Assamese, therefore, became resentful towards the immigrants, especially the more numerous settlers from East Bengal. This resentment found expression in tension, communal clashes, agitations and movements in the pre-independence period.[18]

The situation worsened in the post-independence period, when Sylhet was included in Pakistan, and a large number of Hindu Bengalis migrated to Assam. Even during the British period, a large share of government jobs was held by the Hindu Bengalis, who continued to dominate this sector in the post-independence period. Thus, in the post-independence and of course, post-partition Assam (including present-day Meghalaya), the fertile agricultural lands along the rivers were occupied by the Mymensingh Muslims, the grazing lands in the foothills by the Nepalese, a large share of Government jobs by the Hindu Bengalis, the small-scale retail business by the Biharis and the Hindu Bengalis, and the wholesale business sector by the Marwaris. The series of communal conflagrations, agitations and movements that rocked Assam and Meghalaya since 1979, were primarily attempts by the indigenous community to break this stranglehold and re-establish their control over the resources, as has also been discussed by Das.[19]

The government policies, both during the pre-and post-independence periods, contributed substantially to the generation of social tension in this region. The British economic policy in East Bengal and Assam was governed by what is often termed as the 'frontier attitude', which advocates that once the resources in a given area or region become depleted due to over-exploitation, fresh areas can be explored to meet the demands. Guided by this attitude, which is devoid of an ecological and hence, sustainable concept of use, the British did not adopt any long-term measure to address the problems of land shortage and food deficit in East Bengal. They neither introduced improved agricultural techniques to increase production, nor did they educate the farmers to adopt more sustainable land use measures. They induced the farmer to cultivate jute on all the surplus land, and when this failed to provide the expected fillip to the economy, no steps were taken to restore the fertility of the soil that was exhausted by jute farming. Instead, they encouraged them to migrate to virgin tracts of the Brahmapurta valley, where the Assamese farmers were not in a position to provide them the additional revenue that they wanted to garner. The profits generated by the tea industry were also siphoned off, and not used to build a sustainable economic base for the people of Assam.

Ironically, such short-term and ecologically incompatible policies continued to be followed by the Indian Governments after the independence as well. To illustrate this, some indicative information may be given. The area irrigated as against net sown area in 1981-82 in the North-East was 22.5 per cent, and the per ha consumption of chemical fertilizers (NPK) was 4.2, 9.2 and 11.6 kg. in 1981, 1987 and 1990, respectively.[20] For comparison, these figures were 28.6 per cent and 33 kg. respectively, even in the undeveloped hill areas of Uttar Pradesh in 1981.[21] In 1990, only 15.3 per cent of the gross cropped area in Assam was irrigated, against a national average of 30.7 per cent, and 90.6, 63.5 and 49.5 per cents in Punjab, Haryana and Tamil Nadu, respectively.[22]

As Das [23] has pointed out, whatever agricultural production Assam has so far achieved, has been solely contributed by the natural fertility of the soil and the hard work of the peasants, and not aided by any technological innovations. In spite of having ample reserves of minerals like uranium, coal, lime stone, crude oil and natural gas, and immense hydel power potentials, Assam and the North-East as a whole remain industrially backward. Besides other more well-known factors, the absence of strong pressure groups to lobby for development was cited as one of the most important reasons for this backwardness by the Working Group on Development of North-Eastern Region during the seventh five year plan.[24] However, in spite of its backwardness, Assam had lost 6,200 sq. km. of its forest during 1981-1993, which amounts to about 20 per cent of its total forest area in 1981.[25] The bamboo resources of this region are being depleted to meet the demands of paper mills as far away as in Karnataka[26] while local handicraft languishes. It is only natural that in such conditions, social tensions would be generated, as the different ethnic groups vie for the limited resources available, although the apparent reasons may be far from being resource-related. For instance, the Khasi-Nepali conflict in 1987 was ignited over the formation of a GNLF unit in Shillong although the riot and arson that followed resulted in the eviction of thousands of Napalese graziers and dairy farm owners in different parts of Meghalaya, especially in the Northern *Bhoi* area. These lands were, subsequently occupied by the local Khasis who were facing the problem of scarcity of prime grazing land.[27]

Quo Vadis ?

If, as has been argued in this article, the root causes of communal violence in NE India are ecological. what then ought to be done to diffuse tensions and contain insurgency? Should the fragile ecology of the region be thrown open to the traumas of intensive agriculture and industrialization? No ready answer to such questions can be given, but before arriving at any blueprint for a sustainable development of this region, one should take into consideration the quantum of ecosystem services provided by this region. Ecosystem services are the numerous essential processes like maintenance of breathable air, movement, storage and purification of water, breakdown of wastes and the like, that natural ecosystems provide free to human societies. The relatively uncontaminated and pristine ecosystems of the economically "backward" North-East are providing these services not only to the region, but to the country as a whole. For instance, the numerous wetlands in Brahmaputra, Barak and Manipur Valleys, including the well-known Logtak lake, play a key role in storage and regulation of water flow, recharging of ground water, and purification of wastes. Similarly, the biodiversity-rich forests that conserve soil and water, and harbour various useful plants including those that produce life-saving drugs are among the myriad ecosystem services provided by this region. Intricately interwind with this organic diversity is the rich cultural diversity of the numerous tribes and other ethnic groups that ought to be conserved in an integrated manner. The true economic value of these services are to be assessed by 'Shadow-pricing' and given due consideration while charting developmental plans for this region and making budgetary allocations. In all fairness, funds should be earmarked for conserving these services, and the unemployed of this region absorbed in activities that aim to conserve the ecosystems rather than in those which plan to decimate and destroy them in the name of "development". The hackneyed, run-of-the-mill definitions of economic growth would have to be revised while planning to develop the Indian North-East. Ecological diversity, which in turn comprises organic and cultural diversity, could perhaps provide the buffer systems that would absorb the shocks of social tensions in this turbulent region.

REFERENCES

1. (a) W. H. Durham, *Scarcity and Survival in Central America: Ecological Origins of Soccer War,* Standford, Standford University Press, 1979.
   (b) T. F. Homer-Dixon, J. H. Boutwell & G. W. Rathjens, "Environmental Change and Violent Conflict", *Scientific American,* 268(2): 1993; 16-23.
   (c) N. Middleton, *The Global Casino: An Introduction to Environmental Issues,* London, Edward Arnold, 1995.
2. W. H. Durham, *Ibid.*
3. S. K. Bhuiyan, *Anglo Assamese Relations*: 1771-1826, Gauhati, Dhas, 1949.
4. A. Guha, *Medieval and Early Colonial Assam: Society, Polity, Economy,* Calcutta, K.P. Bagchi & Co., 1991.
5. L.P. Pathak, *The Land-hungry Immigrants: Goalpara the Gateway to Mymensinghias in Assam Valley,* Shillong, North-Eastern Hill University, 1991.
6. S. Nag, *Roots of Ethnic Conflict: Nationality Question in North-East India,* New Delhi, Manohar Publications, 1990.
7. A.C. Sinha, *Beyond the Trees, Tigers and Tribes: Historical Sociology of the Eastern Himalayan Forests,* New Delhi, Har-Anand, 1993.
8. P. Nayak, "Unbalanced Agricultural Development in North-East India", *Journal of Assam University,* 3(1): 1998, pp. 24-32.
9. S. Nag, 1990, *op.cit.*
10. A. Guha, 1991, *op. cit.*
11. W.W. Hunter, *A Statistical Account of Assam,* (Vol. I), London, Trumber & Co., 1897 (Reprint), New Delhi, B. R. Publishing Co.
12. B. Sarmah, "The Pre-Colonial Agrarian Scenario of Assam : Transformation and Crisis" in Raha M.K. and Ghosh, A. K. (Eds) *North East India: The Human Interface,* New Delhi, Gyan Publishing House, 1998, pp. 179-305.
13. W.W. Hunter, 1897. *op. cit.*
14. S. Nag, 1990, *op. cit.*
15. B. Sarmah, 1998, *op. cit.*

16. S. Bose, *Agrarian Bengal: Economy, Social Structure and Politics—1919-1947,* Cambridge, Cambridge University Press, 1986.
17. L.P. Pathak, 1991, *op. cit.*
18. S. Nag, 1990, *op. cit.*
19. G. Das, "Migration, Ethnicity and Competition for State Resources : An Explanation of the Social Tension in the North-East India" in Raha M.K. and Ghosh, A.K.(Eds), *op. cit,* pp. 307-323.
20. (a) A. Gupta, "Ecological Aspects of Sustainable Development in North East India" in Deb, B. J. (Ed) *Regional Development in North-East India : Issues and Prospects,* New Delhi, Reliance Publishing House, 1995, pp. 190-197.

    (b) North-Eastern Council, *Basic Statistics of North-Eastern Region,* Shillong, NEC Secretariat, 1987.

    (c) P. Nayak, 1998, *op. cit.*
21. T. S. Papola, B. K. Joshi, "Demography, Economy and Environment in the Development of Hill Areas of Uttar Pradesh" in Singh, J. S. (Ed), *Environmental Regeneration in Himalaya : Concepts and Strategies,* Nainital, The Central Himalayan Environment Association and Gyanodoya Prakashan, 1985, pp. 187-195.
22. S. Chatterjee, "Prospect of Agricultural Development in Assam : with special reference to Rice Development" in Deb. B. J. (Ed.) *op. cit.,* pp. 135-144.
23. M.M. Das, *Peasant Agriculture in Assam,* New Delhi, Inter-India Publication, New Delhi, 1984.
24. P. Baishya, "Industrial Development of the North-Eastern Region: A Study in Regional Imbalance", in Deb. B. J. (Ed), *op. cit.* pp. 173-184.
25. Centre for Science and Environment, *The State of India's Environment: The Second Citizen's Report,* A. Agarwal & S. Narrain, (Eds), New Delhi, Centre for Science & Environment, 1985.
26. G. Das, 1998, *op. cit.,* pp. 307-323.
27. (a) P. R. Ehrlich & A. H. Ehrlich, *Healing the Planet,* New York, Addison-Wesley Publishing Co., 1991.

    (b) J. Cairns Jr., "Determining Desirable Levels of Ecosystems Per Capita", *Journal of Aquatic Ecosystem Health,* 2 (1993), pp. 237-242.

7

Insurgency and the Hill Tribes of North East India

Chinmoy Kanti Biswas

Insurgency is an inner hostility with weaponry resentment of an organised youth group against the established government and the privileged section of civilians according to their considerations. The insurgents may belong to either majority or minority ethnocultural or linguistic groups who have some specific problems which they want to solve by way of fulfillment of their political aspiration.

The hill-insurgencies in the North-East are mostly turbulent along the tribal belt of the frontiers inhabited by the people of mongoloid origin. The areas are covered with hills, mountains and tropical forests demarcated by international borders of Tibet, China, Mayanmar, Bhutan, Nepal and Bangladesh. To comprehend the nature of hill-insurgency in the North-East, it is essential to examine and understand the cultural history, geographical situation and the economic problems and the struggle to retain the cultural identity within the political and cultural sovereignty of the Indian Union. Except the Bodos and some other tribes of Assam and Tripura, all other tribal groups inhabit the hills and mountainous region. Therefore, insurgency here appears to be more among the hill tribals inhabiting the hilly zones of these states. The most well known insurgent groups of the hill regions of the North-East are:

1. National Security Council of Nagaland (N.S.C.N.) of K & I Group.
2. Kuki National Army (K.N.A.)
3. Hmar People Convention (H.P.C.)
4. Tripura National Volunteers (T.N.V.)

5. Dimasa National Security Force (D.N.S.F.)
6. Mizo National Front (M.N.F.) (now outdated) etc.

The insurgency problem in the North-East is not a post-Independence phenomenon. The threat existed even during the British period. But the British paid little attentions to problems and prospects of these people, because the life and living of the hill people were least beneficial to the political interest and economic prospects of the British empire as a whole. So, they left the people as they liked without disturbing them much. But when the place and people of North-East India came functionally within the map of independent India all the tribal problems specially of hill areas came into light. The waves of pan-Indian non-tribal culture brought about change in the socio-economic life of the people which disturbed their self-reliance, self-dependency, resulting in problem of maladjustment. To get rid of such unfavourable and intolerable circumstances they, instead of looking for a peaceful way, took resort to weaponry resentment against the established government and held the pan-Indian civilians responsible for their misfortune. They also aspired for the political solution of all their problems by way of separating their identity and interest from the rest of the Indian Sub-continent.

Although the socio-political emancipation, territorial autonomy, cultural revivalism etc., are the main essence or ideology of different insurgent groups, there are some common problems which are unique to the entire hill people and these are enough to generate such discontent. The salient problems may be identified as follows:

1. Geographical isolation and cultural alienation.
2. Problem of subsistence economy.
3. Problem of exploitation by others.
4. Feeling of being ousted by other cultural groups.
5. Problem of lopsided developmental measures and maladjustment.

1. In the past the mongoloid people of the North-East India migrated from the neighbouring countries of north and south-east Asia across the hills. Their cultural continuity still remains stretched across the border in the other parts of neighbouring countries and they are maintaining their communication and relationship with the people of those parts rather than with the people of rest of India. Taking such opportunities the

neighbouring countries, having unfriendly relationship with India, provide them with weaponry assistance, training facilities as well as asylum for fugitive insurgents in order to keep the situation turbulent. Over and above, the geographical isolation cuts them off from the Indian cultural mainstream. It creates a gap of understanding and exchange of views and ideas which generate suspicion and hatred and thus stimulate the violent situation. This undue generation of suspicion and hatred between tribal and non-tribal societies deprives the tribal people of the benefits of modern technolgy and scientific achievement. Still they do not tolerate any interference from outside agencies.

2. It is a known fact that the subsistence economy of the hill people of North-East India is mainly *Jhum* or shifting cultivation. It is a devastating system of forest economy. It demands a vast area of deforestation every year with limited seasonal yield. The natural resources on which they can subsist are also limited and the economy is again restricted by reserved forest protection rules and regulation. The imbalanced growth rate of population *vis-a-vis* resources have been pushing them towards the crisis line of the economic subsistence.

3. The hill people of North-East India belonging to the so-called tribal culture are simple minded people with simpler ways of socio-economic life style and simplicity in intellectual exercises, having honest faith and blind confidence on counterparts of economic interactions. Taking the opportunity of such simplicity and ignorance some dishonest businessmen of non-tribal communities often try to exploit them. They purchase the commodities from the tribal people at a cheaper rate keeping them unaware about the market value. On the other hand, the non-tribal dishonest businessmen sell their commodities of inferior quality at a higher rate by hawking from door to door. The tribal people do not know the market situation due to their inadequate communication facilities. When they realise the exploiting situation it aggravates jealousy and hatred against non-tribal communities.

4. Since the Independence the socio-political situation of the country has been changing rapidly. The impact of such change has been felt very much in North-East India with the population migration and influx of population from the neighbouring

states. The increase of population density in the plain areas of North-East is also exerting pressure towards the hill regions. The people from plain areas stretching their habitation to the vicinity of the habitation of the hill people, are capturing their forest or hill economy. So the hill tribal people are faced with competition and threat of their livelihood. It makes them anxious and annoyed with the outsiders. Such autagonistic feelings, ideas and views against the outsiders are bewildering the social psychology of the hill-tribals and stimulating the spirit of insurgency as a means to find the way out.

5. The Government of India as well as the State governments plan for the welfare and prosperity of the tribal people of North-East. Exhorbitant amount of money is being sanctioned and spent in every plan for the purpose, but little is coming to the real benefit or development of the people concerned. The reasons for the non-flowing of the Government benefits to the grass-root level of the hill societies may be multifarious, some of which are mentioned below:
   (i) As a result of modernisation, an economic hierarchical class structure has evolved even in the so-called classless societies of the tribals. The tribal leaders with a bit of modern learning and awareness, having comparatively better-off economic backgrounds, try to exploit their fellowmen by capturing the Government benefits and facilities, keeping others unaware of these. So the benefits do not reach the grass-root level in a symmetrical way and the condition of the majority of the people remains unchanged and deplorable.
   (ii) Secondly, inadequate knowledge of the economic planners and bureaucrats about tribal culture and societies, specially of their social psychology make the plans futile and non-operative. As for example, our Government has established many schools in tribal areas to educate them but such effort proves to be unfruitful as it produces some half-educated angry young men who neither can fit in the traditional economic life nor can they engage themselves in white collar jobs or business because of the limitation of scope in such non-industrial societies. So these unemployed youths hold the government or the modern socio-

economic system responsible for their misfortune and take to the path of insurgency.

(iii) Other instances of futility of government's benefits due to inadequate and improper planning may be cited. The Government has undertaken schemes for the establishment of health centres, water supply plants and settled housing in the tribal areas for their development, without considering their socio-economic way of life. The hill tribes of North-East India are mostly shifting cultivators who shift their habitation from time to time with the changing of cultivable plots. So without having any suitable alternative to their existing economic life, there is no use for the above mentioned benefits provided by the Government.

(iv) The Government has established L.P. Schools to provide primary education to the grown up children in almost all the tribals villages of North-East. But it is an acknowledged fact that the children do not go to these schools in spite of all motivations, like supply of mid-day meal. The fact is that, the tribal economy in hill areas necessitates almost equal labour of all age and sex groups to sustain their livelihood. The grown-up children remain engaged in looking after the children and households while their parents go for out-door work like *jhumming,* collection of fire-wood and forest products etc.

In this way imbalanced and improper planning made without taking into consideration all aspects of tribal culture by the planners who are not conversant with it, make the entire endeavour a worthless one inspite of all amenities supplied by the Government.

(v) Above all, the general and well-known factor for hindering government's efforts for economic development of the hill people is the dishonest and unfair means practised by a section of employees involved in the functioning machinery in distributing government benefits and implementing developmental measures at the grass-root level.

It seems to be easier to identify the problems from different angles than to prescribe and implement the procedures for handling the problems. However, attempts may be made for giving some directions for handling these problems from sociological, psychological and other points of views, as the problems are quite complex and acute.

The insurgency problem is not only a law and order problem nor is it a problem generated from socio-economic and socio-political malpractices alone. Rather it is the product of various adverse situations. So, to handle this problem all aspects and perspectives are to be taken into consideration and the preventive measures are to be taken by both the Government and non-government agencies collectively.

It has been observed that, hill insurgencies of North-East India are being specifically steered along the international border. The insurgents are getting direct or indirect support from the neighbouring countries who maintain a hostile attitude towards the Indian Republic. So, it is necessary to install as strict vigilance along the international border and in addition to that our foreign policies are to be reviewed to revive the warm and friendly relationship with the neighbouring countries in order to stop the continuance of foreign support to the insurgents.

All care should be taken to check the social tension and economic crisis and implement measures to eradicate socio-economic imbalance in the hill societies while formulating the socio-economic planning. It should be realistic and relevant to existing socio-economic perspective of the tribal economy, ecology and corresponding culture. It should not be something imposed upon. It should be some thing evolved through long experiments undertaken and experience gained by the specialists interacting with the tribal societies.

Before the implementation of any developmental scheme, a pilot project in socio-economic study must be carried out by the tribal specialists to understand the realities, their problems and communicate their first hand knowledge of the place and people to planners at the Centre. Accordingly, need based measures are to be devised. In this connection, co-operation from the departments of tribal studies, tribal specialists and voluntary organisations which have intimate relations with the corresponding tribal societies may be sought for. The first and the foremost job is to acquire the confidence of the people so that they may realise the sincerity of the purpose, otherwise the developmental measures may not be acceptable to them and the developmental projects may not yield any result.

The law and order situation of the sensitive areas should be reviewed time and again and legitimate, hard, prompt and responsible actions should be undertaken to tackle any adverse situation. But while taking such actions caution must be taken to consider the humanitarian aspects and to uphold the socio-cultural value system of the societies concerned. No innocent person should be oppressed by any means which may devastate or dilute the objective or purpose.

In order to make attempts to solve the socio-economic problems the tribals youths may be trained in vocational studies. Suitable alternatives to their traditional way of economic life (*i.e.* shifting or *jhum* cultivation) should be identified and successfully substituted. In this regard, priority should be given to the provisions of self-employment utilising the local resources. This may lead to a settled economic life without disturbing the natural surroundings. In this regard, cottage industries may be improved to support their economy. The raw materials and appliances may be provided through government subsidies. The marketing facilities of their finished products are also to be ensured by the Government agencies to get real value of the products. Small scale industries may be set up in tribal areas by utilising the local resources, natural or agricultural. Hydro-electric power projects may be installed on fast rushing wild streams of the areas so that cheap electricity may be made available for the small scale industries of these areas. Thus, the tribal youths may get the scope of employment.

To rescue the tribal people of the interior areas from the economic exploitation of the dishonest opportunist non-tribals some departmental stores may be established by the government to enable the people to purchase the commodities at a reasonable price. It should also have the provision to get the local commodities sold and provide the tribals with reasonable value of their products.

In order to spread general education among the hill people of North-East emphasis should be given on the informal education system irrespective of sex and age. The main objective of the mass education should be to make people acquainted with reading, writing and arithmetic which may serve the purpose of communication and exchange of views with the outside world. The formal institutional education may be continued in a parallel way for those who are dedicated to it and can support themselves intellectually for higher education. They should be ensured with proper employment opportunities after the successful completion of their studies. Instructors for informal education can be appointed from within the community who have adequate qualification and training. Intensive vigilance should be maintained on the function of both formal and informal education system.

For promoting health services, mobile medical team may be appointed to visit the tribal villages as is being done by some voluntary organisations. The educated tribal youths may be trained in first-aid services and homeopathic practices, so that they may tackle the health problems at the initial stages in their area. Road communication should be maintained on a priority basis, from village to village and to the nearest health centre, and the health centre should remain well equipped.

It has been comprehended that the insurgency problem of the hill people of North-East is not at all an isolated problem and is not only economic or emotional in nature. So to handle it, in addition to the socio-economic and other developmental measures, socio-political previews are also to be evaluated. The hostile leaders should be brought unconditionally to the table for open discussion in order to know the grievances of the people and let them know the limitations of the Government in the matters of fulfilling their aspiration outside the frame work of the Constitution. Logical suggestions may be invited from the insurgent leadership to meet their grievances within the Constitutional frame work.

Some positive steps may be taken in the Government net-work and electoral politics, so that no unpopular person is nominated for leadership of the tribal people and is not backed for being in power in an undemocratic way. The Election Commission as well as the political parties should remain cautious so that money and muscle power do not play any role to dictate the political fortune of the hill people by taking advantage of their poverty, ignorance and simplicity. Only then the insurgency problem in the hills of North-Eastern region may be solved to a considerable extent and peace restored.

8

Insurgency in North Cachar Hills

Tanmay Bhattacharjee

The British administration in India did not interfere in the internal administration of the North Cachar Hills district (NC Hills) up to 1854. But an atmosphere of insurgency in the region brought them directly into the fray and they spent the early years combating the struggles directed against the British rule, such as, the Naga rebellion, the Kuki rebellion and the Dimasa uprising. Haflong, the present headquarter of the NC Hills was an outpost to monitor the movement of insurgents in the hills.

In the NC Hills, the uprising against the British was largely influenced by outside factors, such as acts of insurgency in Nagaland and Manipur. Sambudhan Phonglo, the legendary Dimasa leader's revolt in 1882 and his attacks on Maibong and Gungjung as sudden were small company of the Kuki militia was employed to guard Gungjung sub-divisional headquarter. The militia failed to protect the station and the followers of Phonglo ransacked it. However, the success achieved by them was short-lived. The British, in an attempt to tackle the problem established Kuki pockets in the areas bordering the present states of Manipur and Nagaland as a counterpoise to incessant Naga raids in the heartland of the NC Hills. Moreover, the failure of Phonglo's uprising and isolation of the hills greatly helped in keeping a semblance of peace and the problem of insurgency appeared to have been tackled during the British rule.

North Cachar Scenario: The Socio-Political Milieu

The NC Hills always had a composite population with no numerically dominant group. The tribals—Dimasa, Naga, Kuki and Hmar use

'Haflong Hindi' for communiction. Nonetheless, due to historical antecedents, the Dimasas are considered the original inhabitants of the land. Political tension or violence was on a low-key if not non-existent even during the tumultuous days of the eighties. Political awareness or participation was at a low level. In order to ensure popular participation in the developmental process Autonomous District Council was constituted but as the events show, it did not yield the expected result. Politics in the region veers around a few prosperous families with headquarters at Haflong. The ownership of lands in the interior is largely in the hands of these urban elite's. *Jhuming* is done on the hill slopes. Thus, politics and economic prosperity cannot be separated in the region. Ever since Independence these families belong to the Congress party though floor crossing for political and personal gains is not uncommon.

The Dimasa Students Association (DSA) was not a very active organisation even during the early eighties but the failure of the Congress party to involve the youths in its organisational activities and the working of the District Autonomous Council created a feeling of disenchantment in the minds of these youths. Consequently, their earlier aloofness converted into hostility.

The growing influence of the Diphu-based party, the Autonomous State Demand Committee (ASDC) also contributed towards the process of disenchantment.The ASDC in Karbi-Anglong was a cadre based party and had already enjoyed a spell of power in that district. Gradually, a section of the youths in the NC Hills was lured away by the autonomy demands of the ASDC. Its office was established at Haflong. It gradually built up a cadre, recruiting the dissatisfied local youths in the district.

To counter the influence of the ASDC and DSA, the ruling Congress party encouraged the formation of a parallel organisation, All Dimasa Students Union (ADSU). The demand for *Dimaraji* (Dimasaland) was specially raised.

The Dimasa Security Force (DSF), a terrorist outfit was propped up which maintained contact with the similar terrorist outfits operating from the bases outside the district. The Dimasa after the independence were estranged continuously from the main milieu. The tribal population in the district is divided religion-wise into two camps: Hinduised Dimasas and a section of the Jemes (followers of the Haraka Movement) and the Christian Hmars, the Kukis and Jemes. The effect of the Naga Kuki rivalry or the activities of NSCN can be traced even in the NC Hills.

The Dimasa frustration is all too apparent. The tribals are not used to competition on all fronts and when they are asked to do this they feel restive. The growth of population within the district due to the migration of tribes from outside has squeezed the manoeuvering space for them. NC Hills was their 'labensraum' which is now open to competition from other tribes. The Dimasas do not find a comprehensive solution to their difficulties.

District Autonomous Council

More than the inter-tribal rivalry the root cause of the problem in the region can be located in the functioning of the District Autonomous Council. The Council has become a monolithic power structure denying the development of village administration. The traditional tribal village institutions still linger without much support from the Council. There is no attempt to gear up the village administration with a decision making power. As a result, village headmen see the Council as a dole-giving organisation. The Council, on the other hand, seeks the help of these headmen at the time of election; decentralization of powers still remains a far cry.

The traditional tribal set up was village centered ruled by the headman. It was elaborately designed to serve specific purpose and was self-sufficient. The headman along with his officers performed specific duties and looked after the village requirements. In the present context, this set up can serve useful purpose because people have faith in it.

Unfortunately, the normal administration in the region suffers from the ills of over-bureaucratisation, which is against the norms of tribalism. The employees have been appointed much in excess than what is permissible. Large numbers of teachers are appointed in the primary schools and the Council is not able to pay all of them. Similar situations can be seen in other offices where higher posts are created without having any link with the need of the district development. This results in the draining away of the developmental funds resulting in the frustration of the local educated youths. The main reasons for the shortcomings in the District Autonomious Council can be cited as follows:

i) Postponement of the District Council election:
ii) Absolute corruption at the top level.
iii) Neglect of financial management, such as, disparity between resources and expenditure.

iv) Neglect of youths who wanted attention of the elders.

Trouble started in 1992 when the election was due for the Districts Council but was postponed and this process went on every six month. The reasons for such postponement ranged from the non-completion of the electoral rolls to the deterioration of law and order situation. Finally, the election to the Council was held on June 3, 1996, owing to great pressure from the opposition. The election result was a blow to the uninterrupted position of the Congress party in the Council. The ASDC came to power with a thumping majority bagging 15 seats out of 24 seats, the Congress secured 2 seats and 6 seats went to the independent candidates. The ASDC was particularly successful in the Dimasa dominated areas, which indicated that the Dimasa people were largely disenchanted with the Congress Party in the hills and they wanted a change of guard. But the postponement of elections for a long period definitely cost them a great amount of popularity. For the Congress party or for every political party in this sense, the lesson is that it should nurture the youths. When they are ignored, trouble starts. The aging Congress leadership in the district did not have any answer in the face of the youth upsurge.

In Karbi Anglong, in a similar situation (1977) the ruling party was defeated due to this type of neglect shown to youths. It is still not very clear what would be the political agenda of the ASDC in the hills. The people in denouncing the Congress party in June 1996 election had sent some hidden message that they should go for a general consensus for development. Inter-tribal feud is emerging where army was ruling for so many decades. Law and order matched by equity and justice may give a sense of peace in the hills.

The Beginning of Insurgency

Dismasas are peace loving people, not used to taking extra-constitutional means unless driven to that extreme by inimical forces. The power at the District Council became an all important issue and it was to be preserved for the ruling elites at any cost. The insurgent groups from outside like NSCN had wanted local co-operation for a long time and they received it around 92-93. The clandestine support they got from a small section of Dimasa youth was a shot in the arms of the insurgents. At least shelter they get in the hills.

The State police was grossly inadequate to combat the insurgents who get sophisticated arms supply from across the border. Before their link up with the Dimasa outfit, the NSCN had relations with the

Hmar insurgents operating in the District. In order to spread fear in the minds of the people and exert their presence, these groups send ransom notes to individuals. Failure to meet their demands leads to the recipient's death. To cite an example, one officer in the State Agriculture Department, Bichitra Nath was shot dead in the office on 1-3-94 at Haflong because he did not honour the ransom note from the insurgents. However, the culprits were never apprehended. The Government was too afraid even to hold a condolence meeting for the deceased. Insurgency had not only benumbed their limbs but also their intellect. When big officers run out of the district on getting such letters from the insurgents, it is the subordinates in the offices who run the administration. When the subordinates get the notices, the administration comes to a standstill. Thus, under such situation funds slated for the welfare have gone down the drains during the last few decades. The North Eastern Times in its report on August, 19, 1995 mentioned 'Fear psychosis grips residents of NC Hills'. People allege that the GPRNWA was demanding from the business units, Government officials and political leaders amounts ranging from 1 lac to 4 lacs.

The situation has become grim over the years. Normal Government functions have come to a standstill with no solution in sight. Welfarism the professed watchwords of the Indian democracy, has lost its meaning. The various insurgent groups rather took it as a source of their income.

It is understood that these groups have their mentors in the countries across the borders. It is an attempt at destabilising the North East. Small tribal groups in the district would not be the beneficiaries at this game. But to secure peace in the district, relentless effort should be made to establish the 'Rule of Law'. The so-called economic plans, which generate consumerism, should be avoided. The emphasis should be on meeting the demands of the people like food, shelter and education.

Conclusion

Insurgency in the hills has spread its tentacles throughout the district and no area is safe for the ordinary people. The credibility of the office goes down to the lowest level when the employees are not sure to get their pay regularly from the Government. The extortionists have put a parallel economy. The Central Government, perhaps for political reasons, may extend more powers but the organisation is not capable of running its show and its resource base is fast depleting. In 1996, a memorandum of understanding was signed between the Government of Assam and the Dimasa leaders extending more power to the District

Council. However, in the absence of strong financial base, the power extended to the Council proved to be meaningless.

As mentioned earlier, insurgency in the NC Hills is directly linked with the events in Nagaland and Manipur. If that connection was absent the insurgency would have fizzled out before gaining momentum in 1992. The political parties, for their own personal gains encouraged 'disquiet' in the hills.

Nagas with whom peace in the NC Hills is much connected are a dauntless dexterous and assertive people. Unlike the Jeme Nagas, the Angamis and Tangkhul Nagas are not the inhabitants of the place. The Jeme Nagas have good relations with other local tribes. Nagas, divided as they are by dialects and kin affiliation are living in widely scattered villages, which are separated by hills, forests and streams. Honest fellow feeling and camaraderie exhibited within the village are often transformed into deadly rivalries when it comes to inter-village matters. They are fiercely independent and do not tolerate any kind of subservience. Inter-tribal feuds are all too frequent. The American Evangelical Mission made great efforts to covert them to the new faith. The NSCN uses the term 'Nagaland for Christ' in their emblem. It seems to be a conscious effort on their part to strike at the dominant Sanskritic group present here. Clearly, religion is being used to establish unity among them and also to show how different they are from others.

The absence of an idea of accumulation and capital formation keeps the people at the low level of poverty. They do not go beyond the subsistence level. The extreme economic hardship has its manifestation in the socio-political fields. Yet people at the grass-roots do not want violence to continue and want peace to come. The recent effort of the Naga leader of 'Hoho Council' for peace was a move towards this direction but the NSCN spurned the idea. Their goal is complete independence.

Finally, it is emphasised that it is unethical and improper to spend so much of money on the development in the region when it is known that this money is literally 'drained away'. Instead, the Government should put emphasis on the development of infrastructure facilities like roads, irrigation, water supply and electricity.

This situation has also put before us an important question—whether the present constitutional provisions are adequate to meet the growing aspirations of the people. Hence, system evaluation is an important aspect. One may suggest that some sort of Swiss Executive System can be tried in place of the present system. Tribal groups may be represented in the Executive body on the basis of population percentage. The office of the Chief Executive can be held in rotation. This may help in reducing the inter-tribal tension as each group may be assured of a position on the basis of rotation.

For the purpose of electing their representatives each tribal group may be permitted to follow their own system. In this way undue tension in the region may be minimised. This prescription holds valid for the States of Nagaland and Manipur too. If peace returns to Nagaland, NC Hills would be a peaceful place to live in.

NOTES AND REFERENCES

1. Ashikho-Daili-Mao, *Nagas, Problems and Politics,* New Delhi, Ashis Publishing House, 1992, p. 186.
2. *Census of India : Assam* 1923.
3. Dutta, Debabrata : *Cachar Records' Compilation,* 1972.
4. Telegraph, Calcutta, 18.7.1996.

III ~ Insurgency, Human Rights: Towards A Counter Discourse

9

Universalism and Relativism in Human Rights

Problematique of Minority Rights in North East India

Rajesh Dev

> "Indeed Human Rights, viewed at the universal level, bring us face-to-face with the most challenging dialectical conflict ever: between "identity" and "otherness", between the "myself" and "others"...between the universal and the particular, between identity and difference."
>
> —*Boutras Boutras Ghali*

Albert Einstein while addressing the Decalogue Society of Chicago maintained that the ideals concerning the conduct of men toward each other and a desirable structure of the community have been conceived and taught by enlightened individuals in the course of history. These ideals and convictions have resulted from historical experience and from a craving for beauty and harmony.[1] The most important ideal that has concerned all men and philosophies over space and time is the one that allows more freedom for the true efflorescence of human personality. These ideals which allow for the removal of restraint and compulsion on full development of an integrated responsible personality have been referred to as 'rights'. Rights are a result of the social and political struggles that mankind initiated to achieve an order that does not debase the human personality by putting undue fetters on his freedom and affront to his dignity. Human Rights is a set of rights, which involves the recognition of the ultimate worth and dignity of the human individual. This belief in the inherent dignity of the individual has led to the belief in the equality of man. Human Rights, therefore, concerns a belief in the equal dignity and brotherhood of mankind.

The ideal of Human Rights has been crystallised through centuries of socio-historical development. This ideal which visualises man as the highest truth is the subject of great epic like the Mahabharata in India, of thinkers like Confucius in China and of the ideals enunciated in European history during the Renaissance and the Reformation. These ideas and ideals were not constructed self-consciously under any ideological rubric or classification, but were a contribution to the debate and concern that knew no ideological frontiers,[2] and were directed to the overall concern for liberty, freedom, and order in society.

The essence of these ideas and ideals are similar in all cultural domains. In other words, though it is true that man exists in a particular cultural context, he is not exhaustively defined by this culture alone. Human nature ensures that man does not become a mere prisoner of any cultures, but asserts his personal dignity by living in accordance with the profound truth of his being.[3] This assertion of his 'personal dignity' reflects his quest for a higher truth and relation with the human whole. Human Rights seek to embody this quest for envisioning a human whole.

The Problem

Today, as we await our encounter with a new millenium we are confronted with the possibility of moving towards the next stage of human civilisation with a crisis that emanates from gross violations of certain ideals that 'humanity' embodied. Human Rights has been one of these and hence the violation of Human Rights and the possibilities of their redress is an area that invokes our single-minded attention. Any vision that we see of the new future social order must be grounded on a proper negotiation of this crisis, and its non-settlement will ultimately threaten the bedrock of human existence.

Nelson and Green say that though the rhetoric of Human Rights provided a basis of agreement among nations to support Human Rights, the range of definitions of the term and the variety of examples illustrating restrictions on the rights of human by the same nations reflect hypocrisy, fraud, chaos or simple confusion.[4]

The crisis that Human Rights claims confront today is mainly laced with allegations of ideological and cultural imperialism. Criticism regarding Human Rights violations by nation[s]-states are met with stiff opposition, harping on the differences in culture and therefore the inability of the criticising State or the international community to comprehend the cultural context in which the alleged violation is instantiated. Consequently, it is maintained that what is good and what is bad for a particular human being always depends on or is relative to something about his/her context or situation, and something that is never true about the situation of every human being.[5] Towards that end claims and counter-claims are volleyed between the relativists and the universalists; between 'alleged violaters' and 'destined upholders' of the Human Rights concerns.

In order to erase the cobwebs of doubt regarding Human Rights concerns, we have to move back in time to the recent past, to a past when the concern for Human Rights was an overriding need for all nations across cultures. And the dynamics of international politics with differences in ideological orientation obliged the world community to enact a wave of rights in the form of the 'First, Second and Third generation' rights.

The first generation rights were 'traditional liberties and privileges of citizenship', and were the result of the consolidating liberal democracy and its procedural institutions. The second generation rights constituted what were referred to as 'socio-economic claims', and were mainly incorporated due to the increasing oppositional pressure of socialism. The third generation rights which constituted 'solidarity rights of communities, rather than individuals', were at the moment of incorporation, meant to help in the emancipation of the newly emerging nations from colonial bondage.

Today however, on the one hand we find that Human Rights as propagated in the normative claims of the Universal Declaration is susceptible to interrogation in various parts of the world as a hegemonic programme of the western liberal order. And this allegation regarding the ideological thrust of Human Rights is contradicted by an unprecedented violation of fundamental Human Rights and freedoms throughout the world.

On the other hand, we encounter the interrogation of the 'first and second generation' Human Rights by the relatively new category of rights, we referred to as 'third generation' or solidarity rights.

This paper views the former allegation as the result of a set of mutually reinforcing political practices perpetuated by some States against others in a unipolar world together with the overriding 'romance of the nation[s]-state'. On the one hand, we have States using Human Rights as international weapons and on the other, this hypocritic stand is provided as an excuse, by culpable States, to counter claims of political and other Human Rights oppression by harping on the concept of 'internal soverignty'. Explicably, the emergence of a unipolar world led by the United States and its 'liberal' allies has resulted in Human Rights being used as an instrument for settling bilateral and unilateral differences among 'nation[s]-states'—differences resulting not only from ideological opposition but also access to economic possibilities. Human Rights has become the chosen battle-cry of U.S. worldwide propaganda, used as a tool of U. S. foreign policy against States, which hold contradictory views. Human Rights has become a vehicle for the imposition of the hegemonic aspirations of the United States.[6]

Therefore, today we bear testimony, at the operational level, to the fact that, Human Rights which resulted from the European Enlightenment, the independence struggles of the Western hemisphere, the insight of the Enlightened of different cultures and nations and the bourgeois revolutions in Europe is immisered by the U. S. in its use of Human Rights as a tool in its "political language" [Henry Kissinger] and "humane interventions" under NATO.[7] This has provided culpable States to allege about the 'non-universalist' inflections of universal Human Rights.

The second concern regarding the interrogation of second and third generation rights by the communical or 'solidarity' rights—which forms the focus of this article—is the result of a mixed bag of fallouts. The third generation or solidarity rights which were initially meant to exorcise the third world and some socialist countries from their colonial fetters, are being abused by communities within both the worlds (after the collapse of the second world)-third and first—as well as between the third world and first world. In other words, solidarity rights are being operationally mobilised at two levels. First, internationally between 'sovereign states' and second, internationally, at the level of communities residing in 'sovereign states'—communities who are said to be privileged by virtue of their indigenous status within the particular nation[s]-states. The fundamental difference between the third and first/ second generation rights is the emphasis on the communal and non-individualistic character of the former.[8] This article views this interrogation of the 'civil, political and economic' rights by the rights of communities as an instance of relativism that today seems to have shifted the focus of attention from universal 'Human Rights' violations to particularistic considerations of such.

The debate between the relativists and the universalists has its roots in the contradictions and divisions of liberal philosophy. It is argued that contemporary liberalism enunciates an individualism that is incompatible with the questions of group and cultural rights. Liberalism propagated by writers like Rawls and Dworkin requires revision to make room for group rights.[9] According to thinkers like Kymlicka, contemporary liberalism assumes a cultural assimilation and homogeneity among citizens which is difficult to obtain. This critical tension of liberalism, wherein it tries to negotiate cultural specificity together with universal homogeneity has been the source of the current paradox in Human Rights. Contemporary liberalism is said to negotiate questions of cultural specificity with a tacit belief in the ultimate homogenization of peoples and cultures.

This critical tension in liberalism is not a recent phenomenon and gets reflected if we merely rummage through the various definitions of rights and the concomitant Human Rights. On the one hand, we have thinkers like Horowitz who concur, "a common legacy of democratic and social assistance of libertarian and egalitarian frameworks is the assumption that there is such a goal as human rights.[10] On the other hand, we have thinkers like Alisdair MacIntyre who claim that there are no [human] rights and belief in them is one with belief in unicorns and witches.[11]

These quotations reflect not merely the definitional variations among liberal theoreticians but also initiate doubt regarding the epistemic and ontological foundations of liberal 'rights' or 'Human Rights'. Consequently, we encounter philosophical infirmities concerning the constitution of Human Rights. The casualty of these philosophical infirmities and definitional contradistinctions are discontinuities in the practical operation or practice of Human Rights through out the world today.

The palpable lack of praxix between theoretical principles and political practice emerges from this critical tension in liberalism. Liberalism granted group rights premised within a compromise between the universalist urges and particularist orientations, but it was equally optimistic that 'differences' among peoples will be erased once all acquire a semblance of civilised 'industrialised' existence. Hence, as a goal, it promoted the process for the strengthening of the universalist orientations of mankind but, as a political strategy, kept ensconced their particularist emotions.

Consequently, this dualism and lack of similarity and sincerity between the goal and strategies of the liberal order has made us incapable of implementing Human Rights as a universal category of rights transcending national and international boundaries. Universal Human

Rights were perceived as a category of rights which shall overcome our bounded realities of State and Nation. This has not been possible and, the Universal assumptions of Human Rights seem repeatedly vulnerable to the particularisms of both Nation and State.[12]

Universalism-Relativism: The Liberal Tension

These diametrically opposite pulls have resulted from the fact that Human Rights as practised and propagated throughout the world today is a child of the instrumental reason of Western Enlightenment. The 'civilising mission' of the West forced upon the rest of the world, which did not possess that reason, these ideas regarding Human Rights. Today however, the presence of independent nations with different cultures and specificities led to the questioning of these ideals which are said to be reflective of western values and ideals only. Despite the fact that in most of the countries we find the operation of a western liberal system of governance and incorporation of its procedural institutions and development strategies, simultaneously the formation of consequent values. These betray similarity with the western model.

Therefore, initially we have to identify the contradictions within the liberal philosophy itself and then confront the possibilities of the relativist pulls of cultures. The primary contradiction in the liberal tradition is to be traced to its assumptions regarding the universality and particularity of human reason and rationality. In liberal philosophy many thinkers maintained that rights emerged and operated in the context of the distinctive national traditions and legal orders,[13] and thereby objected to any universalisation of rights. This also implied that human reason and rationality operated within a contextual reality. However, during the Enlightenment and its subsequent spread throughout the world in the form of a cultural baggage of colonialism we encounter attempts to provide a universal grounding to the category of rights. This marks the beginning of that phase of liberal history when the exigencies of economics dictated philosophical presuppositions. The progress of the 'civilising mission' through colonialism undermined all those ideals that the liberal philosophy preached. Freedom acquired a very restrictive scope and Human Rights slowly got established as positivist principles utterly divorced from morality and ethics.

This liberal tradition of undermining the universal fundamentals of human existence got sharpened with thinkers like MacIntyre and Rorty who question the 'foundationlist' assumption of rights and consequently a universal category of Human Rights. These thinkers derived philosophical inspiration from thinkers like Burke and maintained that human reason is context-dependent and Human Rights are grounded in that reason. Hence, Human Rights are context-dependent as well. More simply, they call for the enunciation of a culture-centric pedagogy of Human Rights. However, what was really needed was the interrogation of restriction in the scope of freedom of groups and individuals that came along with Enlightenment and not the Universalist presuppositions. The emergence of a global world with deep interlinkages and 'diffused sovereignties' runs counter to this philosophical strand that inevitably argues for compartmental states and cultures. It is beyond doubt that the absence of a universal category of rights and a more universalist international body shall increase possibilities of its violation in the absence of international pressures.

Besides these internal pulls of the liberal tradition reflecting the tension, the Marxist tradition identifies the liberal conundrum in the very essence of liberal rights. Marxist literature implies that Human Rights as practised in the liberal world are claimed from a possessive individualist ideology and are claimed by individuals against the power of the State. This, therefore, reflects the antagonism between the rights of man and the interests and authority of the State.

This possessive individualism makes an individual's dignity and self-realisation dependent upon ones muscular and self-assertive capacity to limit others.[14] Thus, the Marxists identify the inherent fallacy of Human Rights as the one emanating from the very source of the individualist liberal tradition and the nature of the liberal-capitalist State. According to this school of thought the conundrum regarding the universalisation of Human Rights can be traced to the very essence of the possessive individualist philosophy.

Further, within the liberal tradition Human Rights at the operational level, concern rights which are linked more to the political and social sectors and Human Rights concerns emanating from depravities of the economy are attributed peripheral significance. It, therefore, neither considers as appropriate Human Rights questions emerging from structural inadequacies, nor does it propose to mitigate them.

For the Marxists, however, Human Rights is only an epiphenomenon and the social structure is the phenomenon, and hence, any analysis of Human Rights has to be ordered by an analysis of the social structure. Thus, Human Rights as a separate discourse within the Marxist tradition does not gain much currency.

Universalism—Relativism: Cultural Tension

The "Universal Islamic Declaration of Human Rights" further aggravated the tension between the Universalist and particularist notions of Human Rights. This Declaration sought to question the western ideals of Human Rights. The Islamic countries, in announcing this Declaration brought into close scrutiny the role and intentions of an international body like the United Nations which, though it is a result of an ideal that is universal in vision and sought to overcome our bounded reality of nations and states, reflected bias for western principles and practices. These countries maintain that the UN interventions, in many countries including theirs, on the questions of Human Rights not only constitute violation of their sovereignty but also imposition of 'western' values. This relativist stand regarding Human Rights, more or less, pursues the pattern set by those liberal arguments questioning the universality of Human Rights, and the need for culture-specific rights.

However, despite the allegation of philosophical and operational infirmities the 'Universal Declaration of Human Rights' of 1948, made an universal affirmation that Human Rights should not be distinguished on the basis of race, colour, sex, language, religion, political or other opinions, national or social origin, property, birth or status. This claim of the Declaration is based on the assumption of the inherent sacredness of the human being, which is assumed to transcend philosophical infirmities, ideological oppositions, operational contradictions, and cultural restrictions. The Declaration reaffirmed the universal vision of the brotherhood of mankind and sought to revive the metaphysical and moral claim to a transcendent human existence and by acknowledging the inherent sacredness of the human being recognised the unity of human dignity. Besides the above, today we encounter the truth regarding a new type of cultural particularism or relativism emerging from an insular awareness of one's own nation, ethnic or tribal community.

Here, the relativistic nature of Human Rights gets reflected in the fact that only those individuals are considered sacred who belong to one's own nation, ethnic, or tribal group.[15] In a sense, the intensity and egoism reflected in this awareness defies the very tenets of the Universal Declaration. The increasing straightjacketed awareness of one's ethnicity and its insular theorisation and consolidation coupled with the challenges and depravities of economics, threaten to further strain the possibility of a universalisation of Human Rights. The contemporary social philosophy's schism regarding any form of foundationalism provides theoretical rigor and sustenance to this 'relativistic facade' of ethnic groups and communities. I mention this as 'relativistic facade' because this relativistic position is brought to operation only as an act of counter mobilisation to questions concerning serious violations in social, political and other sectors. As an instance, while acknowledging the fall in the moral fiber of mankind in general the ideologues of thèse ethnic and tribal groups reflect their Universalist inflections. In other words, they show cognisance of the fact that there are sectors which transcend ethnic and other considerations. However, when it concerns Human Rights, which is nothing more than a general agreement on the fundamentals of human existence, the question of cultural specificity overshadows all humane considerations.

Another fundamental feature that emerged alongside this relativism is the fact that Human Rights emanate only in relation to the State and are of no concern in inter-community relations. In short, collective or solidarity rights are invoked selectively by communities to address Human Rights violations of selective communities and cultural groups. This will be clearly demonstrated when we discuss the Indian dilemma. Another consequence of this relativism is that Human Rights concerns are removed from the domain of the civil society and are transposed upon the State which is assigned the final authority for arbitration and protection of Human Rights, reinforcing thereby its positivistic features.

However, inspite of these claims and accusations, at a macro level the doctrine of Human Rights as practised and propagated around the world today affirms the fundamental principles of western liberalism with its contradictions. In most of the countries with little variation we have western liberal democracy as the system of governance. And the liberal tradition has developed with the belief that every individual is to be treated as an end in himself and hence articulates concerns centering individuals and their rights. It is not only true that these countries have accepted all the contradictions of the liberal philosophy by way of adopting the system of governance, but have also increased the amount of contradiction due to the presence of their own peculiarities and specificities.

Further, the identification of new disadvantaged groups in consolidating liberal democracies led to the justification for the granting of special rights in order to achieve equal citizenship. Hence, we find that modern liberal States accept the special category of collective rights and appropriate methods of positive discrimination to remove arbitrary disadvantages and discrimination. This at a theoretical plane does not seem to be confronted with any contradictions. In fact, the concepts of individual and collective rights have a similar history and a similar general rationale. Individuals and collectivities have been oppressed throughout history and in the modern period protection has been sought in the form of institutionalized rights.[16] However, it is true that this concern for collective rights has evoked international concern for collective groups, but it has also stimulated abuse of 'collective rights' for making unreasonable and destabilising demands, which contradict common criteria of citizenship, based on universal civil and political rights.

The Indian Dilemma

Considering the above as a theoretical backdrop, we may look into the conceptual and operational contradictions that arise when we consider the developments in any multi-ethnic State including that of India. In these countries contradictions arise because of the lack of explicitness in the legal concepts and also their political instrumentation by ideological groups.

India adopted a system of governance that reflects similarity with the dominant western liberal ideology. Hence, it also incorporated all the provisions and principles of the individualist liberal philosophy despite the fact that the liberal individualist philosophy had only been imposed by British colonialism. Consequently, when the western-bred intellectuals and thinkers settled to adopt a written constitution they showed very little regard for the ancient civilisation or any of its principles. They imposed a system on a group of people who were not fully equipped to undertake the travails unleashed by a system incompatible to their cultural past and political practice. The half-hearted synthesised version of a Constitution, which is assumed to recognise some of the aspects of their cultural past made compatible with the structures of the western model produced immense anomalies that today threaten to question the very integrity of the State. Despite being the biggest democracy conforming to its western principles it sustains a fragile stability and is confronted with a future, which reflects indeterminacy.

All this leads us to reflect on the inadequacies that were responsible for the non-settlement of the "revolution of rising expectations"[17] not only in the economic sphere, but also in the cultural and social as well.

Majority-Minority Relativism

One of the most pertinent areas that seem to attract our attention is the fragile stability between the 'majority' and 'minority' groups. India being a multi-ethnic State required utmost care in developing a system of governance wherein the 'minorities' could have a better participation in the decision-making process. However, the terms 'majority' and 'minority' have been beset with problems. The history of the country has been such that minorities in functional terms mean only the religious minorities. In fact all major theoreticians have implicitly referred to 'minority' and 'majority' within that structure. For example, theoritician like Asghar Ali Engineer implicitly, without clearly defining the terms majority and minority—structured his writings within that premise. Even the political agencies have premised their political agenda in such terms. However, sociological terminologies refer to 'majority' and 'minority' not merely in the numerical sense. To exemplify, the case of blacks in Africa and women in the United States are usually cited to highlight the fact that though they constitute majorities in their respective areas they are the subordinates by virtue of their inability of influence and participation in position of power. Therefore, the suggestion by Yetman to think of majority as a synonym for dominant, and minority as a synonym for subordinate[18] seems to be helpful in our analysis of the dynamics of the Indian imbroglio. Because not only do we have numerous groups which are numerically superior but subordinate in terms of receiving social resources but also due to a federal structure their numerical quantity may vary from State to State. Majorities and minorities can also be determined by such other factors as ethnicity, race, religion, lifestyle and sexual preference. Hence, though it is true that at the national level, we broadly bifurcate majority and minority through religious affiliation, it is afflicted with numerous contradictions. We are a country with numerous religious, ethnic, and linguistic minorities. Therefore, clear constitutional connotations regarding the concept, taking into view the facts that the 'dynamics of relations between majority and minority groups are in most ways similar' and that it is not a group's numbers but its role that makes it a majority or minority, must be implemented.

In India, we encounter, consequently minority groups, which are varied and multilayered. Initially, as we have already done, it is necessary to identify broadly the first group of minorities in terms of their religion at the national level.

The creation of linguistic States made an implied reference to the presence of other minority groups—the linguistic minorities, groups who were less numerous than either the dominant national linguistic groups or the States they hitherto identified with. Linguistic States were meant to protect and promote the cultural heritage of these differentiated peoples. The consequence of accommodating the increasing demands of different ethnic groups and their call for separate statehood led to the creation of a second set of minorities—linguistic minorities—a process through which the hitherto national minorities became regional majorities.

The quagmire about who constitutes a minority does not stop here. The identification of historically disadvantaged groups and the enunciation of positive discrimination to ensure justice implied the existence of another group of minorities—backward minorities. Minorities who may be linguistically and religiously differentiated but constituted a minority by virtue of their disadvantaged positions.

We, therefore, not only encounter different layers of minority towards whom academic attention has not been provided either due to ignorance or political correctness but have also unleashed a process wherein many of the minority categories overlap, providing some with a double-edged advantage.

Further, the constitutional terminology as to who constitutes a minority has been ambiguous leading to further confusion. There has not been a clear identification and articulation of this legal concept in the Constitution, which forms the bedrock of numerous legal and constitutional benefits granted to citizens. This initiates ambiguity in legal and political discourse and subjects the concept to instrumentation in political agenda. And the supposed inflections of the Constitution, on this legal concept require constant interpretations of the Supreme Court. Despite many references to minorities and its constant interpretation found in the national and international instruments, a generally acceptable definition capable of universal application has been elusive. The clear lack of consistency in its definition both at the international and national levels to the evocation of all sorts of claims.

At the international level, the Permanent Court of International Justice made efforts at describing the term. Various other international forums kept up their efforts at providing a clearer understanding of the term. In the Indian case, the landmark judgment of the Kerala High Court was supposed to provide the much-needed consistency to the term and settle the ambiguity of the Constitution. The Court observed, "in the absence of any special definition we must hold that any community, religious or linguistic, which is numerically less than fifty percent of the population of the State is entitled to the rights guaranteed by the Constitution"[19] However rather than solving the inconsistency the judgment initiated counter claims keeping in view the federal structure and the presence of numerous linguistic States other than the national state.

In other words, the judgment did not specify the ambit of the term 'State'—whether it meant the State of India or its constituent units that are also referred to as States. This was either because the Honorable Court took it for granted that 'state' in the Indian case meant only the State of India thereby undermining the position of the federating states and reinforcing the centralist tendencies or it wanted to steer clear of any political improprieties. Whatever be the intention it did scanty little in resolving the controversy.

As maintained earlier, the national minorities became regional majorities due to the granting of linguistic and ethnic states, it simultaneously reduced many of the national majorities into regional minorities in these linguistic States.

It led to the emergence of another group of minorities within the constituent States—regional minorities. And though the Constitution guaranteed rights to all citizens throughout the territory of India, it simultaneously envisioned overlapping claims of certain communities to exercise exclusionary rights over their territory. To be more precise these constitutional guarantees led to a form of closure[20] on the part of certain cultural communities, ensconsed under conditions of 'rough' equality. It also undercut the necessary democratic social and political consciousness among the 'people' where citizens could look upon their fellow citizens as equal, legal and political beings.

More so some areas were granted the rights of denying access to citizens from other parts of the country. These constituted areas dominating the northeastern periphery of the country and were composed mainly of the tribal people who were otherwise the dominant majorities of these states. They were deliberately kept separated under a facade, which can be articulated as 'Nehruvian dualism'. This dualism was made on the plea that these areas should be allowed to develop according to their own genius. However, the real intention of the leaders might have been the unwillingness of negotiating with a contingent exigency that emerged due to the apprehension of these areas regarding their role in the new union. The compromise led to the granting of benefits like the Fifth and Sixth schedules. Today most of the dominant groups inhabiting these areas have been granted their own states, wherein all their rights and freedoms have been more or less ensured and protected.

As in all other multi-ethnic states, in India as well, we confront the dilemma of identifying groups which can claim rights on the basis of their minority status and minority encapsulates all ethnic, religious, and cultural divergences. Therefore, minority should be identified keeping in view the disadvantaged position of groups residing within that state—disadvantage in terms of the prevailing power symmetrics.

There is no doubt that the communities at the helm of decision making in these peripheral linguistic States can be considered minority in terms of their position *vis-a-vis* the State of India. But for the other communities inhabiting the State who do not constitute the dominant group, a clear articulation of legal concepts is imperative, and is linked to their enjoyment of rights and realisation as full legal citizens of these States.

Heuristic Solution

This implies that in any multi-ethnic State with a federal structure but with a single citizenship and existence of communities other than the dominant ethnic groups in the federal states the question of 'minority' has to be treated as a multi-layered phenomenon. A holistic identification of a minority in any multi-ethnic state with federal governments can prove hazardous for the minority that is constitutive of that particular federal State.

The national State has to reconcile or transcend the diversity by the incorporation of credible institutional interfaces and political will guaranteeing equality. This requires objective delineation of the formal legal concepts.

In these pheripheral states of India there is an element of distrust, hatred and closure among the dominant and non-dominant ethnic groups, coupled with the denying of certain fundamentals of humane existence to the 'minority groups' who are not part of the dominant ethnic groups. Minorities in the northeast India are variegated and some of them are yet to acquire historical antiquity, which seems to be the most valued criteria for making communities indigenous and hence they still remain as a wounded scab that erupts with the slightest scratch. In these States those violations are supported and legitimated as Human Rights—by the State and the civil society—which are considered to violate the rights of the dominant ethnic groups. Grave violations of such basic rights as right to life and dignity of the non-dominant ethnic groups receive no opprobrium from the society and may even be said to receive tacit state approval.

Instances of violation of the Human Rights of the non-dominant ethnic groups are numerous. An instance, in the state of Meghalaya, which has a matrilineal society, is the violent rape and consequent gory murder of a non-dominant ethnic lady in 1992 during the yearly saga of communal clashes, which did not evoke any criticism from the dominant civil society. In the same State the spitting on the coffin of non-dominant ethnic but Christian lady also failed to evoke criticism from the dominant society.[21] These instances reflect the tendency of the dominant community to deny sacredness to a community other than its own[22] and the result of which are aberrations in the enjoyment and implementation of Human Rights.

More recently, a division bench of the Gauhati High Court in a judgment directed the Government of Meghalaya to hand over to the Central Bureau of Investigation the investigation into a series of lynching cases of August 1998 that had left at least eleven persons dead, most of the victims belonging to non-dominant ethnic communities.[23] Though these instances are merely routine criminal activity and no immediate communal intentions can be ascribed, the pattern of the violations, including the partisan attitude of the law-enforcing agencies in recording and investigating cases of sustained violence against the non-dominant ethnic communities reflect communal bias and undermine the fundamental freedoms and exercise of legitimate rights of the minority non-dominant communities. In fact the directive of the High Court reflect lack of trust in the investigating agencies of the State. In most of these States the very construction of a 'community' reflects exclusionary tendencies and the historical role of violence[24] in such a community construction has been deliberately ignored and sidelined in picturing the organic development of the indigenous communities. Echoing Bipan Chandra we may even say that the inhabiting communities perceive a dissimilarity and divergence in their social, cultural, economic and political interests and these interests are also antagonistic, mutually exclusive and incompatible. These interests thus acquire communal overtones in the State where the non-dominant ethnic groups are not only religiously contrasting to the dominant groups but are also categorised as 'non-tribals'—different from the 'tribals' who constitute the dominant group. It further implies that communities non-constitutive of the dominant group are not sacred and are hence unworthy of claims to be treated at par so far as enjoyment of fundamental freedoms are concerned.

Rights have come to imply and endorse the egoistic and selfish nature of man against one another. They no longer imply positive expressions enabling people to realise their potentials reflecting their reciprocal dependence and sanctity for each other's self-respect and dignity. Rights have been utterly divorced from their concomitant duties. The dominant ethnic groups by virtue of constituting the national minority constantly question any constitutional and legal intrusion into its social and cultural arena on the pretext of they being violative of the minority rights guaranteed by the Constitution and the International Declarations. Under this particularistic and relativistic position it becomes convenient to even push aside the basic tenets of the Universal Declaration, which sought to look at humanity first and then the constituent collective and minority groups which make that humanity.

In most parts of the world today this placing of the cart before the horse has unleashed grave dangers to the needs of the human society for a proper category of Human Rights. This inverted justification of collective rights may at one time jeopardise the very essence of liberal Human Rights, unless everyone is made aware that rights of one is inextricably linked with the rights of the other and entails consequent duties on each one to respect the rights of the other. Undue emphasis on the technicalities and particularities of national, ethnic and cultural pride and its relation to the question of justice may lead us far away from the search for harmony, order and consequent consideration of rights.

Conclusion

The relativist challenge to the idea of Human Rights is not plausible, because of the fact that human beings are all alike in some respects that support generalisations both about what is good and what is bad, not just for some human beings, but for every human being.[25] This, therefore, leads to the identification of universalist assumptions for at least some ways of life which are bad and horrific and some ways of life that are good for every human being. However, it must be acknowledged that there is no one way to truth, it is negotiable. In other words it is to say that, "there are many important respects in which human beings are not at all alike", emphasising the pluralist conception regarding human good. This realisation regarding the pluralist conception of good however, does not dissuade us from acknowledging certain universalist values like 'affection, co-operation with others, a place in the community, help in trouble'[26] which are in reality the core considerations of any Human Rights agenda. It is also inarguably true that there are many and various forms of human excellence which will not fit together into one harmonious whole,[27] or even that there is any determinate feature or set of features that eliminates all but one ideal as valid,[28] but the conditions necessary for the pursuance of these excellences and ideals are in most ways similar.

The Human Rights agenda delineated in the Universal Declaration does not call for the elimination of difference between truths but only endeavours to negotiate a conception of human good, that is, and should be, universalist as well as pluralist: it acknowledges sameness as well as difference, commonality as well as variety,[29] because as Walzer maintains, though in a slightly different context, that the only plausible alternative is humanity itself.... entire globe. Therefore, any Human Rights agenda must, as a fundamental premise, consider the aspirations of the human whole as its first and foremost guiding principle.

However, there is no denying the fact that Human Rights have today acquired a clear ideological thrust. This is not the result of the incorporation of the liberal political values into the Human Rights agenda but primarily because of the hedonistic practice and symmetry of power which has received new thrust due to the collapse of a multipolar world.

Also, today the Enlightenment tradition is under tremendous onslaught from 'anti-foundationalist' traditions. These traditions interrogate the 'agenda of Enlightenment' for undue emphasis on collating all human knowledge under an Universalist umbrella. Hence, they also question the legitimate result—the 'Universal' Declaration. However, if we question the attempts of Enlightenment tradition for its undue inflections towards universalism, we can criticise the anti-foundationalist traditions for its undue emphasis on the relativity of ethnic, cultural and other specificities, and also for falling into the same circularity of identifying collective disadvantaged groups under an universalist rubric by implying similarity in their disadvantages, intensions and aspirations. These 'anti-foundationalist' traditions can be accused of ideological piracy, in the sense that they are coating the growing economic disparities, within and between nations, by emphasizing the insular primacy of culture. Today more than cultural hegemonisation we face the onslaught of an unhindered and hedonistic economic hegemonisation with changed characteristics and renewed subtlety of vigour.

However, it is a fact that there is a thin line that divides the universal attributes of man and his relativist orientations. Therefore, it does not seem to be an easy task to negotiate the confrontations between universalism and relativism in human rights discourse. However, to a great extent this relativism can be narrowed if legal concepts utilised by constitutions of national states are clearly articulated taking into consideration the fact that though modern states are a far cry from their idealised positions of 'nation-states', they are also no 'mono-ethnic' states.

It may not be wrong to conclude that an analysis of the contradictions, reveal that Human Rights are still an amorphous concept that emerged because of some inherent utopian tendency of humanity towards achieving a higher stage of existence and order. Human Rights is an agreement on the general principles of human existence governed by maximum freedom for the efflorescence of human personality and has been necessiated due to frailties of humanity reflected in the scourge of the two world wars.

Unless we are able to resolve our contradictions based on specificity of culture, ethnic differences and national boundaries, we shall remain incapable of negotiating the consequent crises that emerge in the philosophical postulates and political operations in the concern for Human Rights. The consolidation of a universal category of Human Rights will not be possible within the bounded realities of our present existence, an existence where an international body like the United Nations remains merely an ideological appendage.

And the consequent contradictions that emanates in imposing such a boundless idea like human rights, which transcends limit of territorial and cultural frontiers and ideological differences, gets reflected in the history of human rights as disparity, "among general principles, variant definitions and contradictory practices"[30] rendering it difficult to implement the Human Rights agenda as a common collective monument of the aspirations of humanity.

NOTES AND REFERENCES

1. Albert Einstein, *Ideas and Opinions,* Rupa paperback, 1995 p. 34.
2. Jeremy Waldron, *Liberal Rights* (collected papers 1981-1991), Cambridge University Press, 1993 p. 36.
3. Noam Chomsky, "*For Reason on State*" 1973 cited in Michael Perry, *Human Rights Quarterly,* 1997.
4. Jack L. Nelson & Vera M. Green, *International Human Rights: Contemporary Issues,* N.Y. Human Rights Publishing Group, 1980. p. vii

5. Michael Perry, "Are Human Rights Universal? The Relativist Challenge and Related Matters", *Human Rights Quarterly,* 1997, Vol. 19, p. 472.
6. Uwe-Jens Heur & Gregor Schirmer, "Human Rights Imperialism", *Monthly Review,* Vol. 49, March 1998 p. 5.
7. *Supra,* pp. 5-6.
8. Jeremy Waldron, *op cit.,* p. 341.
9. W. Kymlicka, *Multicultural Citizen,* Oxford, Clarendon Press 1995.
10. Irving Horowitz, " On Human Rights and Social Obligation", *Transactions: Social Science and Modern Society,* Vol. 15, No. 1, Nov-Dec-1977, pp. 26-27.
11. Alisdair McIntrye, *After Virtue : A Study in Moral Theory,* London: Duckworth 1981 p. 67.
12. R. J. Vincent, *Human Rights and International Relations,* RIIA, Cambridge, 1986, ch 7.
13. Edmund Burke, cited in David Beetham, *Political Studies,* Special Issue, 1995, p. 1
14. Jeremy Waldron, *Nonsense upon Stilts : Bentham, Burke and Marx on the Rights of Man,* London, 1988 p. 196.
15. Michael, J. Perry. *op. cit.,* p. 462.
16. Richard Thompson, "Ethnic Minorities and the Case of Collective Rights", *American Anthropologist* 99(4), 1997, pp. 786-798.
17. Adlai Stevenson cited in R. L. Hardgrave jr. *India : Government and Politics in a Developing Nation.* 1979, p. 1.
18. Norman R. Yetman, *Majority and Minority : The Dynamics of Race and Ethnicity in American Life,* 4th Edition, Boston 1985 p. 1.
19. Kerela Education Bill, *AIR* 1958.
20. Michael Walzer, "The Communitarian Critique of Liberalism", *Political Theory* 18, No. 1 1990, pp. 6-23.
21. *The Shillong Times,* Oct 1992.
22. Michael J. Perry, *op cit.*
23. *The Shillong Times,* March 1998.
24. Veit Bader, "Citizenship and Exclusion", *Political Theory,* 23, No. 2, 1995, pp. 211-246.
25. Martha C. Nussbaum, "Compassion: The Basic Social Emotion", *Social Philosophy and Policy,* 27, 1996, p 744.
26. Phillippa Foot, "Moral Relativism," in J. W. Meiland & M. Krausz edits. *Relativism : Cognitive and Moral,* 1992, pp. 152, 164.
27. Bernard Williams, *Ethics and the Limits of Philosophy,* 1985.
28. David B. Wong, Moral Relativity, 1984, cited in M. J. Perry, *op cit.,* p. 472.
29. Stuard Hampshire, *Two Theories of Morality,* cited in M. J. Perry, *op cit.,* p. 473.
30. Nelson & Green, *op cit.,* p. vii.

10

State, Insurgency and (Wo)man's Human Rights

Two Cases from the North-East India

Sukalpa Bhattacharjee

The early conception of the 'rights of man' in the seventeenth century and the subsequent international idea of 'Human Rights' in the twentieth century as explicated in the Universal Declaration, had the male household in mind.[1] Human Rights or 'rights of man' were conceived as rights of each individual against the other and rights especially against the government which ruled them. It was generally assumed that there existed a *private sphere* of the family protected by rights from intrusion from outside but it was not necessary that rights of members were preserved within that *private sphere,* where maximum number of human rights violations take place. In many countries, it has been seen that a woman's most insecure and dangerous space is the 'home' she lives in, and I would, in a broader sense, extend it to the ethnic community. The public/private dichotomy ushered in by the institutions of modernity has made the sphere of 'home' or 'community' a more volatile space with the assumption that 'right to privacy' of the male household is the right to do whatever the male head wants. Under Article 12 of the Universal Declaration, 'rights' become a double edged word for the 'male' to isolate the gendered subject in a more private sphere where she can be fully exploited without official intrusion from outside. It reads "No one shall be subjected to arbitrary interference with his privacy, family, home or correspondence..."[2] One should mark the gender specific word 'his' in this Article. Article 16 of the Universal Declaration of Human Rights which is devoted to marriage and family, naturalizes the heterosexual two parent patriarchal model. Therefore, any rational analysis of 'Human Rights' and appreciation of all 'beings' as human cannot but begin with an interrogation of the institutionalising of Human Rights and the male bias in it. Recent growth of feminist Human Rights literature argues for a rethinking of Human Rights and a change of male priorities for women's rights to be fully recognised as Human Rights. Rights of all human beings to exist as 'human' cannot be perceived without challenging the concept of Human Rights and the institutions of family, cultures, communities and religion which serve as the agencies of the institution of Human Rights. At the institutional level, significant development in the direction has been, a petition drive, before the United Nations World Conference on Human Rights held in Vienna in 1993. It was urged that the conference should address women's human rights at every level of its proceedings and recognise gender-based violence as "a violation of human rights requiring immediate action...[3]". This had positive impact on Vienna declaration and programme of action. The Fourth World Conference on Women in Beijing in September 1995 followed this agenda in significant ways.

I

Following my extension of the *private* space of the family to the private space of the (ethnic) community in which gross violation of women's human rights take place, it can be seen that "respecting cultural differnces" has become an euphemistic expression for denying women's human rights within the community. Relevance of the sanctity of cultural practices is evoked on issues of sexuality, marriage and reproduction while the same traditions or rules are conspicuosly ignored in matters of commerce or crime. In countries where religious fundamentalism is the weapon of political power, emancipatory drive of women is associated with 'western' or 'white' values and is therefore, rejected. These values are further accused of being anti-national and anti-religious. One can recall here the case of Taslima Nasreen of Bangladesh. Cultural construction of feminity continues to be the ontological ground for a sexual or ethno-sexual definition of a woman and therefore it becomes an urgent political necessity to re-think human rights as women's rights. Looking at women's rights would mean looking at the institutions of family, religion and (ethnic) community in a new light and contextualizing the cultural rights of women. At least after the American Civil Rights Movement, there has been an awareness of the harm suffered by ethnic or cultural minorities and the subsequent moral claims of these communities to cultural integrity. But the idea of Minority Rights itself is problematic because of the perceived clash between individual rights and group rights which makes the creation of "internal minorities" inevitable.[4] The question of personal autonomy even in the realisation of cultural or political rights of minorities can be at stake as the empowerment of minority groups might lead to the persecution of their own "internal minorities". The gravity of this problem has been one of the bases for the emergence of subaltern histories, which are the histories of the voiceless, historiless, unorganized "internal minorities".

In this article, while making a critique of the patriarchal model of Human Rights, I examine the process of the formation of the ethno-national communities in the North-East at the backdrop of which Insurgency has been shown as an inevitable consequence of the "Nation formation from above". However, the main thrust of my argument is that the gendered subject of the North-East has experienced a 'natural' exclusion both in the process of the nation formation and from the discourse of Insurgency, which claims to have interrogated such a formation. She is an internal minority, who is defined by the multiple categories from which she is excluded—State, Insurgency or Human Rights. Unfortunately, the mainstream feminist over-generalisation of 'patriarchy' and the inside-outside role of feminist social critics had not taken care of the ethno-sexual positions in ethnic and tribal societies. Amidst Ethno-national claims of 'saming' and 'othering' and in the tension of inter-ethnic conflicts, it is the (wo)man, on whose body violence is deeply inscribed. In countering the hegemony of power of the Indian State, Insurgency does not succeed in overcoming the logic of power. It is a game of power which in its patriarchal essence is neither philosophically liberating nor is politically revolutionary.

It is violence or power-thrust for the hegemony, of either the State or Insurgency, because both have statist agenda in which the (wo)man is conspicuously absent. The ethnic woman of the north-east suffers the imposition of the ethnic males regarding preservation of traditional customs and costumes during ethnic movements, mostly without a decision of their own. She is only a giver because in the patriarchal game of power, she has nothing to gain. On the other hand, during army operations by the Indian State she is a silent spectator, as her beautifully kept hearth and home is ransacked, her brothers and sons killed in the encounter in front of her eyes and she is finally abused and raped. Neither the Indian State, nor Insurgency can safeguard the life and rights of a woman because she is the common sight/site for both, for enacting the drama of power and violence. From her position of a twice marginalised subject what is her plausible alternative? Can she go on bearing the violence? Should she articulate a new language of her own, which can re-define her identity as a women rooted in her culture, outside the violent drama of the State and Insurgency? It is interesting to see how a woman of the north-east asserts a female subjecthood through her indirect rejection of the logic of the State and of Insurgency. This assertion constitutes her Cultural Rights as Human Rights, which explodes the interior of the patriarchal symbolic order of her community (in violence) and of the State. She discovers for herself a tradition specific role that secures her a position of a subject within social bonding amidst the social distortions produced by the patriarchal dispositions of hegemony. She does not embrace the agenda of Insurgency irrationally—an agenda that offers no perspective for changing the entire bourgeoise structure of the Capitalist State, but seeks to replace one for the other, which will obviously lead to the same consequence of deprivation and violation of Human Rights. The whole ideal of Human Rights will remain a misnomer so long as the Capitalist State does not whither away. Therefore, the counter hegemonic struggle of insurgent groups only at the level of acquisition of political power, without posing a philosophical challenge to the logic of the Capital, will yield no good to the people. Insurgency becomes a self defeating drive that destroys itself, and its internal minorities especially the 'woman'.

I make a study of two women's organizations of North-East India — The Mizo Women's Federation and the Naga Mother's Association, which are unique examples of cultural refiguration of women and widening of their sex specific roles, which is also a redefinition of their Cultural Rights in the form of ethnicity inscribed on sexuality and vice-versa. These organisations celebrate cultural specificity, within cultural diversity and also interrogate 'cultural excuse' for marginalising women. An important section of women in the North-East seems to have realised that "Patriarchy which operates through gender, caste, class and ethnicity, is integral to the problems facing women".[5] Some women from North-East India have been participants also in the Beijing conference which in an unprecedented manner has rejected "cultural justifications" for violating women's human rights.

II

North-eastern tribes in general never had a defined community as such although their life style was communitarian in nature. The generalised problem of Representation, of the subaltern subjects of North-East takes a critical turn, because the political or ideological embeddings of these tribes were never national or post-colonial. It was rather a partially tinted social space, where certain identities were articulated through an extraneous discursive agency. This process had left the North-Eastern tribes, out of the national metaphor and the colonial national artifacts of power left them as unadjusted outfits. This in turn, produced a difference in culture and at the same time an implied compulsion, of the tribes to make themselves considered within the language of history, thereby attenuating the already disrupted voices of that found articulation in the social space of the tribes. The tribes who were so long kept out of the emerging colonial public space (s), were forced to make a forcible intrusion into the colonial national public spaces — the force of which in turn made them subjects of contingent self-fashioning.

At such a phase, the homing in of Christianity with the residues of colonial liberal western discourse and responses to earthly pathos and disempowered spirituality, paved the way to something demonstrably optimistic. Famines and traditional saviour spirits were all losing ground and vanishing in front of the white man's religion. The cognitive shift of the natives was by way of rejection of the wrecked structure of faith, only to get accommodated within something more strong. This is how the North-Eastern tribes, as subalterns were unconsciously caught within the currents of the dominant discourse, without a decision of their own, yet they were different. With the absence of the artifacts of history / time, memory and an ordered language, the tribal natives in general lacked the agency to appropriate the concealed violence of the colonial ruse. This epistemic violence was also marked by an absence of desire in the tribes to recreate themselves in indigenous artifactual ways of world making. It may be mentioned here that this type of cognitive shift is also visible in modernity, which has language to articulate it, unlike the crisis in the tribal societies which lacked even the language to describe. A sense of community emerged among the natives of the North-East only with the advent of modernity, when a desire arose in their heart to articulate their traditional ecritures into language of modernity. In contesting the always already contaminated space of modernity, the tribes for the first time, started experiencing a 'loss' of their identity which they thought they had, and so each time they tried to 'write' it, it resulted in an erasure (in the Derridean sense). And therefore the community formation here, was a kind of a con-social bonding an intersubjective primordial relationship of sharing, which projected a life-world beyond a community. It was not a political formation of a community like other subaltern communities but an ecological one. Modernity, with its statecraft demarcated life into too many autonomous spheres as private/public, secular/spiritual etc. which started generating a lot of tension in these ecological groups, which were used to a communitarian way of life. These divisions left the realm of everyday life a remainder and so the power relations became more visible in this 'space'. A sense of 'loss' pushed back the ecological community to their traditional way of life, but influenced by a critical modernity, the traditional society started assigning roles to the members of the community.

The power relations operating between individuals with various roles and between communities, arranged multiple identities against each other and brought them to the sites of production, politics and administration. This pattern of rupturing of various self-enclosed identities by the colonial modernity reinforced the dominant-dominated relationship in cultural terms in which one identity perceived others as a threat to its existence. The Indian national discourse operating through such a contest-ridden public space, mediated the intercultural relationship between communities without addressing their specific cultural claims. The abrupt attempt to turn them as individual members of a greater claim of Indian nationhood left cultural spots uncemented and has created dual subjects—'native' and the 'civic'. The 'native' subject could not adjust himself / herself with the dominant imageries and symbols of the Indian Nation because of the 'otherisation' which had constituted it as the 'other'. On the other hand, the 'civic' subject activated its Indianness only in matters of civic interests because in matters of inter-community relations, the traditional and customary institutions were to secure them ethnic rights. This dichotomy transformed the civic sphere into a terrain of unequal competitions because different ethnic communities enjoyed different or no ethnic rights. In the decolonising process of post-colonial India, the dominance of certain communities over others became more clear and so discontent and deprivation became inevitable in the form of Insurgent resistance. In the context of NE-India, the existence of socially rooted dominance in the political space gave way to the claim of various ethnic tribes and communities for separate province and State such as Mehgalaya for Khasis, Nagaland for Nagas etc. These claims and the encountering of the State hegemony of dominance have been termed as Insurgency by the State, which through a mobilisation of national sentiments justifies its violence to curb it.

Thus the North-Eastern tribal societies emerged into ethnic national groups projecting various traditional ways of world making. In seeking to distinguish between individual ethnic cultures, minority discourse and the internal minorities,[6] one finds that the woman is the internal minority—the ethnic subject, with colourful ethnic costumes and gender specific roles. Under various institutions of modernity and the conflict between the 'Minority' (an awareness which is quite recent in the North-East) and the State, the 'woman' becomes an ethnic object under the male 'gaze', — gendered and fetishized. Being an ethnic subject of a community, which has been subject to the process of nation formation from above, the cultural rights enshrined in the Constitution become a misnomer to a woman of the North-Eastern tribal societies. And so, her 'culture' and Cultural Rights are asserted in her celebration of self-reflexivity in carrying out her gender specific roles. In a community which inscribes ethnicity on her sexuality and vice-versa, an assertion of Cultural Rights would mean 'becoming a woman', and as Elizabeth Grosz describes "going beyond identity and subjectivity, fragmenting and freeing up lines of flight, liberating a thousand tiny sexes that identity subsumes under one"[7] In her predicament as ethno-sexual subject, she must celebrate 'a body without organs' (Bwo) as Grosz states, which does not oppose or reject organs but — opposes the subordination of the body to the exigencies of property and propriety. As mentioned earlier the tribal/ethnic woman remained conspicuously absent from the visible spaces of the emerging public spaces of politics and administration. She also remained excluded from counter hegemonic struggle of the insurgent groups. In the play between identity and non-identity and in her assigned traditional sex-specific role, she could not emerge as a subject—'native' or 'civic'. And therefore, from within the cultural system which has metaphorically erased her identity, she has asserted her new-found subjectivity. Let us examine the growth and functioning of two ethnic women's organisation, the Mizo Women's Federation and the Naga Mother's Association, which are operating in a manner, suggestive of a viable alternative to the mal-logic of Statist hegemony and ethnic Insurgency. Their discourse action projects the violation of human rights that ethnic women surffer and how such a fractured subject could gather herself to celebrate her Cultural Rights, which none but she herself can guarantee for herself.

The Mizo Women's Federation, more popularly known in Mizoram as MHIP, *i.e.* Mizoram Hmeichhe Insuihkhawn Pawl was founded in July 1974. The Constitution declares that the organisation would be solely engaged in social welfare works and it would be done by women because "we women also must contribute our share by uniting our efforts towards the accomplishment of this great task". The position is almost an ethical feminist one [8], as the Mizo woman is trying to enlarge the space of her articulation as an ethno-sexual subject struggling to achieve individuation from her gendered role. Her agenda is much more comprehensive than her ungendered counterpart, whose space of articulation is constituted by only a critique of the centre-periphery politics [9] This organization is the largest women organization in the State and all Mizo women are members of the MHIP, irrespective of social and economic position, starting from the first lady of the State, down to the poorest rural Mizo woman. Their aims and objectives include child welfare, women welfare and mediation between the civil society (Government Health & Immunization programmes) and traditional society. A unique feature of the Mizo society is the absence of class, caste, social hierarchy and this aspect has greatly helped the project of the MHIP to unite the Mizo women. The Mizo Women Federation, unlike mainstream feminist movements is not engaged only in exploding the interior of the partiarchal symbolic order. It strategically (consciously or unconsciously) avoids confrontation with the State. It pledges co-operation with the Government programmes of National Integration, observation of Republic Day, Independence Day etc. However, the MHIP's subtle critique of the traditional and modern patriarchal institutions can be deciphered by reading into the organisational text. The MHIP has come up with a very fundamental agenda of the improvement of the Mizo customary law which, according to them, is treating the woman "like domestic animal". The annual report of the MHIP for the year 1994-95 states :

> "The women in Mizoram have no security in life due to the fact that the customary law treats the women like domestic animals. We have no rights to claim our property .... Although the old customary law relating to marriage and inheritance are still upheld, there are changes in some parts of India and beyond".

The MHIP is aware that the Mizos are still at an infant stage of civilisation, none the less they desire to be a part of the emancipatory movement of women and the improvement of customary law in other parts of India. The organisation states that earlier in the marriage system, the bride used to take only her personal dresses and bedding with her from her father's house. But now-a-days, brides from well to do families are taking much more valuable things from their father's house. The MHIP is raising voices against these practices, lest it should become a convention in the society. In a memorandum, submitted by the MHIP to the Chief Minister of Mizoram on the 16th of Oct. '97 at Aizawi, the Organisation has demanded 33% of elected seats and one-third of the Chairperson seats for women in the village Councils and district Councils. Further, the organisation feels that the reservation of 33% of seats for women should not only be in the Parliament but also in the State Assemblies, particularly in Mizoram, which so far has had no woman MP and which has had only 4 women members of Legislative Assembly during the last 24 years. Significantly, the MHIP has urged the Government for the adoption of (a) The Christian Marriage Bill, 1994; (b) The Christian Adoption and Maintenance Bill, 1994; and (c) The Indian Succession (Amendment) Bill, 1994, which will ensure and provide for better security in a Mizo woman's life. It may be mentioned here that in the Mizo Customary Law, the youngest son inherits the property of the father. For a woman there is no certainty that the youngest son would share the property with her after her husband's death[10]. It is strange to note that although Mizoram, (one of the smallest states of India) has high literacy rate, especially of women, the unjust customary law still holds good. It is also surprising to note that the Church, which had taken care of converting the Mizo people to Christianity, remained silent in relation to the implementation of the Christian Marriage, Adoption and Maintenance Act. This demand of the MHIP has shaken the roots of the patriarchal order, both traditional and religious. It is learnt that the Church Unions do not assign higher post to women, who qualify the Bachelor of Divinity and Master of Divinity (BD & MD). It is a clear case of gender discrimination in the Church, when qualified women on Divinity, have to work as clerks in the Church office and the higher posts are enjoyed only by men, who are equally if not more qualified. I have argued this elsewhere, that the Church as another patriarchal institution, still carrying the colonial legacy in certain ways, marginalises the woman. The North Eastern tribal states are mostly Christian, and it is almost a convention that even political matters are imparted in Sunday Sermons in some Churches. The question is, how do the religious institutions maintain a conspicuous silence, when the whole region is burning and bleeding. [11]

The text of the MHIP, seems to be providing for an inter-textual reading of the various agencies of the modern civil society and how the woman is caught in the nexus. The MHIP has declared 1997-1999 as Women's year and is taking up cases of rape, exploitation of women etc., for legal redressal. In 1994, the MHIP organised a big demonstration, when a lawyer's wife (suspected of murder) died. The Organization with the help of the Village Defence force of a larger organization in Mizoram, called Young Mizo Association (YMA, of which both men and women are members), is trying to appropriate various currents of patriarchy operating in a Mizo woman's life. The word MI-ZO means man-hill, a landscape where woman is absent physically and yet it is the woman, who is mediating between the 'man' and the hill, the burden of sexuality inscribed on her ethnicity.

The Naga Mothers' Association, is another organisation of Naga Mothers, who have taken upon themselves the task of projecting themselves as effective citizens. Unlike MHIP which subtly contests the discourse of the traditional and the civil society, the Naga mothers have deliberately kept themselves outside this contestation. They have taken the responsibility of clearing their own homes and repairing the moral cores of the fractured Naga society. The Naga tribe is constituted by several sub-tribes, who collectively assert themselves as a community. The Naga mothers, whose sons are engaged in the battle with the Indian State, act as mediators between their sons and the civil society. Insurgency is a Statist discourse, in which the Naga woman does not involve herself, rather she carries out her role as a mother, who on the one hand prevents her sons from taking liquor and drugs and on the other hand works for ensuring eco-friendly environment. The Naga Mother Association makes individual mothers address the community as social mothers, enlarging the space of the tradition-specific roles. The community as an ethnic identity is not beyond gender consideration and so from her sexed subject position, the Naga mother figures the discourse of motherhood in the community. It is a delicate mixture of the impersonal communitarian entity with the personal female 'self,' almost a two dimensional matrix, in which the community emerges as the limit of the self; a kind of radicalisation of community (radicalisation in the Derridean sense) in the political sense, in the sense of an exterior mobilisation of the responses of the female 'self'.

This role of the Naga mothers is a quasi-appropriated, quasi-neutral role on the face of the coerced and feigned body of the community, which is suffering the predicament of a historical fracture. I call it a radical role of the mothers because it challenges the grotesque, the voir of the State in a voice enundated in a pool of tears and blood. The organisation symbol of the Naga Mothers' Association is very significant; projecting a human eye from which tears of blood are dropping down and a four worded message — SHED NO MORE BLOOD. This is a mediating message both to the Indian State, (with its coercive military force) and the insurgent sons in the NSCN (Nationalist Socialist Council of Nagaland). One interpretation of this could be that it is an intra-patriarchal battle in which mothers are wounded. The symbolic crying eye of Naga motherhood is an unprotected space in the highly protected policing spaces of the civil society. The Naga Mothers' Association radicalises the experience of violence, and its promised disposition towards a negotiated order of peace is the poetics of counter Insurgency that does not debunk insurgency but projects an area of hope. This hope is articulated through a counter ideology of non-violence that could struggle for reclaiming the lost position of Naga identity. It is an attempt of resurgence of a community from its wounds and a memorising enactment of a sense of ethnic bond, which can give birth to a 'nation from below'. The Naga Mothers' Association takes almost a eco-feminist stand, working towards an ecological restoration both of the cultural ethos and of the flora and fauna of Nagaland. Two questions are relevant at this point: Does Naga identity suffer defeat before the Indian State? Does the Indian State bank upon the communitarian capacity of resilience without holding a legitimate moral authority? These discursive questions loom large in the matter of ensuring social justice as an agenda of struggle, more than a prescriptive and normative legal justice.

The matter of social justice assumes priority in the vision of the interiorised community as manifested in women's assertion, with its immediate affront to the legitimacy of the Indian State. An interrogation of the Naga Mothers' Association in this public sphere of the civil society is irreducible to an altruistic or statist move because the stake of the State is jibed with the mistake of the State. How does the civil society adapt itself to this state of affairs? Does it take a legal and constitutional possession or does it leave open the question of procedural justice? The question is, who negotiates between these normative polarities and what prime place do these polarities occupy in the agenda of struggle. Leaving aside the matter of balance of power to the confronting agencies (State *versus* Insurgents), the excluded fractions of the community who feel the pinch of this irresolution between the two, cognise these intricacies and take a radical non-conformist position, the appeal of which attracts both the warring sides. Naga Mothers' movement position itself in the narrow but intricate space with a self-delineated responsibility of recreating the fractured community. In this sense, the Naga mothers perform the role of symbolic authority of motherhood, which is more effective than the real authorities in the traditional society and the visible centres of State power. The women especially the mother is the most affected in the insurgency situation because it destabilises her physically and emotionally and so from a dis-empowered position the mother/woman manipulates the various agencies of State power. Interestingly, the Insurgents and the Indian State, both resist any subversion of the symbolic authority of the mother because neither can manipulate it. Both take recourse to the symbolic authority of the mother because the space of motherhood does not give rise to a dominating centre of power relation.[12]

Thus the two women's organizations, in a manner quite unique and different from the mainstream feminist struggle, configure the cultural role of the Mizo and Naga women respectively. Both the organisations operate with a collective ethos and yet leave the space of individuation of the female (sexed) subject. The Mizo Women's Federation is a case of more effective jerk to the foundation of traditional and modern patriarchy, where sexual identity has been inscribed on her ethnicity with the force of the Customary Laws that makes gender discrimination. The Naga Mothers' Association is a case of an ethnic communitarian role of the mother, who is past sexual youthfulness but who is using her gendered identity as a mother to resurrect the ethnic community. The mother had once been a sex-specific object from which she has emerged as a maternal authority, a responsible citizen and so, the Naga Mother is trying to inscribe her ethnic identity on her sexual identity. I, therefore, read the position of the Mizo and the Naga women in three phases—pre-critical, critical and post-critical. The pre-critical stage constitutes the period when the woman was totally a non-entity in the communitarian stage of the community, when the colonial ruse and the dominant Indian ideology was inflicting violence on the indecisive community. She had no memory, no decision and finally no language of her own. The critical stage consists of that period when, with the advent of modernity, her sex-specific role was assigned to her and she realised her gendered position and the discriminating language game of patriarchy. The post-critical phase is the most significant, almost a post modern cognitive shift of the sexed subject, as she is effectively using the language of patriarchy to contest it and create the language of her own. This is what constitutes her rights as a human being and as a sexed subject in culture, that interrogates the male institutions of power and offers an alternative model for the recognition of women's rights as Human Rights and Cultural Rights.

NOTES AND REFERENCES

1. This idea has been extensively discussed by Susan Moller Okin in her article "Feminism, Women's Human Rights, and Cultural Differences" in *Hypatia* Spring 1998, drawing on other feminist critics.
2. United Nations, 1948
3. Elisabeth Friedman, "Women's human rights. The emergence of a movement" in *Women's rights, human rights International Feminist perspectives*, 1995 quoted by Susan Moller Okin in *Hypatia*, Spring 1998.
4. Leslie Green in "Internal Minorities and their rights" in Will Kymlicka's. *The Rights of Minority Cultures,* OUP, Oxford 1995.
5. About 240 participants from 110 non-governmental organisations (NGOs) in the Asian Pacific region concluded on this note. See Charlotte Bunch's "Strengthening human rights of women" in *World Conference on Human Rights, Vienna, June 1993 :The Contributions of NGOs' Reports and documents* ed. Manfried Nowak ,Vienna 1994.
6. David Lloyd has given a comprehensive account of the problem of ethnic cultures and minority discourse in "Ethnic cultures, minority discourse and the state" in *Colonial discourse/post-colonial theory*, (ed) Francis Barker Peter Hulme and Margaret Iversen 1994; p. 221.
7. Elizabeth Grosz discusses the terms (BWO) and 'Becoming Woman' in her article "A thousand tiny sexes. Feminism and Rhizomatics" in *Topoi* (An International Review of Philosophy) September 1993.
8. The idea is borrowed from Drucilla Cornells' "What is ethical feminism" published in *Feminist Contentions: A Philosophical Exchange*, Routledge, New York and London, 1996.
9. One of the most effective critique of the formation of the Indian State at the initial stages of the transfer of power from the colonisers to the Indians is available in *Ka Ram Leh Kei (My Country and I)* written by R. Vanlawma, the only living political biographer in Mizoram

10. These facts are gathered from MHIP literature collected from their office and from personal interviews with the executive members of MHIP in December 1997.
11. I have argued this elsewhere in relation to the women of the matri archail societies of North-East, who are making themselves productive in the global market, as commodities instead of enjoying a priviliged position of matriarchy.
12. The facts are gathered from fieldwork in Nagaland (Interpretation mine).

11

"Nations from Below" and "Rebel Consciousness"

The "New Subaltern" "Emergence of North East India

Prasenjit Biswas

'Nations from below' are those identities that reinforce their collective and community values by way of a looped counterclaim to the dominant identity that includes it from a distance and from a position of strength. These identities from below attain their autonomous position by way of inverting the claims of dominant nation, that is, by claiming sovereignty, territory and institutional authority for itself. This means a disorientation of the dominant state by launching struggle against the machinery of the State that inducts smaller identities within its fold. 'Nation from below' does not make a claim of Statehood, as 'the nation from above' does by establishing the primacy of the State in asserting its authenticity. The authenticity of the 'nation from below' lies in its parallel counterclaim based on its own cultural distinctness not based on the power of the State.

The counter dominance struggle of the 'nation from below' in the context of NE-India raises the issues of internal colonisation by the Indian State as raised by ULFA and NSCN. What it means is a gradual encroachment upon the national and cultural resources of the ethnic communities to produce a sense of disorientation within these communities reminiscent of a process of colonisation. NE-Indian communities are therefore, sensitive to cases of deprivation by way of privileging the non-ethnic people in the matters of State, who in turn, ensure their dominance upon the State and make it an instrument of marginalising the ethnic people. The resistance to such a process is another characteristic of an emergence from below which pre-empts the possible consequences of dominance of non-ethnic communities upon them.

The mobilisation of a host of reactive and rigid identities that embroil themselves in an interconnected state of conflict forms the plot of originary violence in the process of inclusion of the North-East within India. The colonial State simultaneously pitted such identities against each other and negotiated between them in such a way that the legitimacy of colonialism is not questioned by such identities. One of the important nationalist strategies was to uncover this colonialist manoeuvre and to free the State from banking upon planned civil conflicts. The idea of nationalist resistance was to reconstruct a harmonious civil society by bridging up its internal differences in order to put up a united front against the colonial state. The nationalist forces therefore, had to resist simultaneously the politics of culture played by the colonial State and maintain a united civil society to thwart the hegemony of the colonial State. So far as resisting the colonial politics of culture was concerned, the nationalist line of action was effective, but in their attempt to reconstruct a united civil society they had to go along the already constituted markers of differences existing within the civil society and, therefore, nationalist discourse merely lined up such identities in a counter strategy of containment of the colonial power. The nationalist discourse oriented all its ideas of reconstruction of a harmony between rigidly structured and 'pitted-against each other' identities towards resistance to colonial power. Hence, nationalist appropriation of indigenous cultural resources were affected by the colonial construction of the nation. Rather, nationalist discourse produced an analogous idea of a 'nation' that goes parallel and mimics the colonial 'nation'. This was manifested in their construction of a unified space of civil society that pits itself in a total strength against the totality of colonial power. Nationalist discourse constructed a 'whole' against the 'whole' of colonial power and as such 'whole' constructed by the nationalist discourse was engaged in a diabolic encounter with 'whole' of the colonial power. In counter posing the colonial power, the nationalist discourse got trapped in structuring itself as a perfect alternative, as an alternative type to the colonial power. It was an inverse appropriation of colonial power. In doing so, what the nationalist discourse had given rise to was an unified whole of civil society that could/can mitigate the factors behind the cultural contest among differing identities. Rather the nationalist telos of unity and integrity produced a smug and vague sense of unity, so fragile and transient that it subverted the interior of nationalist discourse. The cultural compulsion of the nationalist discourse to forge unity among contesting communities could not draw them towards evolving a unified civil society but gave them a vague sense of unity against the imposing whole of the colonial power.

This process of constructing a civil society divided between communities on the one hand and negotiating between these communities on the other formed the agenda of the colonial State. In case of North-East India, the creation of Excluded Area, Partially Excluded Area and system of voting based on religion etc., were mooted by the colonial power to reinforce the already existing primordial boundaries between communities. In resisting these, the nationalist discourse of Congress had to devise a strategy of bringing together religious minorities, tribals and dominant Hindu caste groups within its fold and design principles that take care of the interests of each of these blocs. More than sorting into the particularistic demands of these blocs, what Congress was interested in was keeping together all such blocs by a common agenda for struggle *i.e.* struggle against the colonial power. In other words, cultural compulsion of the nationalist forces was dictated by their political compulsion and hence it turned internally self- subversive and conflictual. The nationalist desire to make various communities and blocs a part of the wider system of governance was overarching in character and faced resistance from all those who could visualise dominance through governance The elite nationalist project of hemming in smaller communities under a greater structure of the State became an elitist agenda that left out the possibility of affirming distinctive cultural claims on the part of the constituents of the nationalist whole.

Consequent upon this, historiographic and politico-ethnographic constructions of the native spaces of NE India could not attain a phenomenological validity in terms of being true to the distinct forms of life sustained by people belonging to them through material hardships. Hermeneutical elements in such constructions were never put to any test or authentication matching the intensity of these hardships. It was the hegemonic goal which prompted these constructions. A subversion of this distinctness of the communities of this type was a necessary component of this goal. Formation of a *rebel consciousness* in the ethnic formation was an obvious corollary of this subversion and dominance through governance. An unfortunate and promiscuous consequence of this formation was power acquisition game among different ethnic groups yielding inter-ethnic violence. The State which had no control over this ethnic conflict, rather based its hegemony on such conflict. A play of the ethnic rebel consciousness can be read in certain actions of interrogation of the markers of the dominant metaphor of the Indian nation.

The call for boycotting national days such as Republic Day and Independence Day by the militant outfits from NE India is an attempt to subvert the dominant national imagery. The image of the nation as 'other' projected by militant outfits bring out slogans such as 'We were never a part of India', 'we want sovereignty'. The boycott is a rejection of the process of homogenisation and dominance of the advanced communities though the State assumes them to be subjects of consent of the State. The native and indigenous sense of history endowing the NE Indian communities with different sense of sovereignty and freedom undercut the burden of a sense of freedom from the colonial rule. The native and indigenous sense of history cannot reconcile that sense of freedom from colonial yoke by its necessary conjunction with rise of post-colonial Indian State and thereby problematises both the claim of sovereignty and legitimacy of the Indian State. This problematisation undercuts the normative bonds among communities as prescribed in the rules of the State, which by implication also means an opposition to the socially rooted dominance on which the State bases itself. The ethnic criterion of autonomy, self-subsistence and sovereignty comes as a reactive factor to the dismissal of such criterion by the State and it fashions a different self-identity opposed to the universal national identity upholding the legitimacy of the State. What the ethnic positioning of the 'self' questions is the necessary banking of the Indian State upon a dominant universal self-identity by questioning both such a dominant national identity and its subsumption under/within Indian State. In case of NE India, construction of identities like Zo people spreading beyond Indo-Myanmar borders, greater Naga homeland including Myanmarese Nagas or even construction of a Tai-Ahom nation appropriate territoriality, history and sovereignty in a much different way than the run of the mill anti-colonial nationalist narratives of the 'Indian' kind. The direct opposition between customarily rooted indigenous system of governance and the Indian State produces a sense of marginalisation and apprehension among the native communities of the NE India. This situation necessitates a multiple agenda of struggle against dominance that articulates sovereignty, equal rights, development, secession etc., in order to make a move beyond the limits of Indian State and nationalism.

To account for this articulation of a sense of difference in laying claims of sovereignty, territoriality and community linkages beyond the boundaries of India in the case of NE India, one can clearly distinguish the official statist-nationalism from ever emerging claims of independence and nationhood from native communities. The official statist-nationalism differs from the ethnic-nationalism of various communities in a significant way as it debunks the claim of sovereignty of those communities on the ground of inviolability of the Indian Constitution and indivisibility of Indian territory. The claim of sovereignty of ethno-nations is based upon their distinct cultural ethos, which has never been a part of the sudden recrudescence of the nation-state from the colonial past. The decolonisation that flows from the emergence of the nation-state creates a situation of reaffirming self-identity of such communities in distinct terms and by this they encounter their own allies and aliens, positioning them in a distinctive way. This reaffirmation problematises the priority of the Indian State over their ethnic affiliations and resets the ethnic and cultural domain as prior to the defined limits of the State. This mode of positioning of an ethnic community is a symbolic negation of the superiority and primacy of Indian nationhood, which positions a State above all claims of sovereignty and independence. Indian nationalism in its Statist form blocks the space for alternative claims of sovereignty and thereby produces resentment among the ethnic communities of NE India.

II

What is contested in NE India is both the forging of post-colonial nationalism by selective appropriation of cultural resources of native communities and the Indian State that administers such an appropriation and encodes it as development and democracy for the NE India. But the contest centres itself around the visible dominance of the State created through socially rooted dominance of certain communities, which has led ethnic communities to struggle against both the State and those dominant communities on whose behalf the State supposedly acts against the interests of the native communities. Recent poll boycott call in Nagaland by the apex body of voluntary and village organisations of Nagaland could be interpreted as an example of this contest with the Indian State on the ground that elections are not acceptable unless a solution is arrived at with the militant organisations. Two layers of legitimacy are in conflict here; on the one hand, the authority of the State is questioned by boycotting the legitimate means through which the State holds its authority, and on the other, claims of sovereign citizenship for an independent Naga nation is mooted by such an action. The 'nation from above', the nation which is already constituted and designated by the Indian State is opposed by a 'nation from below' against the perceived dominance of the Indian State in forcing consent upon the 'nation from below'. Quite interestingly, the soft pedalling by the Indian State on the demand for carving out the Naga dominated areas from Manipur to create a greater Nagaland was contested by other communities of Manipur on the ground of their perceived threat of vivisection of Manipur and subsequent dominance of the Nagas. Here the resistance is directed against the creation of Naga dominance and interestingly enough, the Zelian-grong Nagas had also opposed the move to separate Naga dominated areas as they perceived the threat of dominance from other Naga tribes. This many-voiced terrain of community mobilisation against dominance creates a field of resistance for those who refuse to accommodate themselves within the monolith of Statist nationalism. The burgeoning Anti-integration movement in Manipur demanding pre-merger status exhibits a move beyond the limits of Statist-nationalism.

Not only such contestation occurs against dominant nationalist ideology of the Indian State, but the contestation is carried out against the perceived dominance of community in the immediate neighbourhood. The contestation against dominance is carried out at a deeper level, the level upto which the socially rooted dominance is structured and percolated for making possible the emergence of a group identity with counter posing claims of equivalent nationalist feelings. This emergence from below against a hierarchy of dominance structured by the State from above could be called 'nations from below'.

An interesting example of such an emergence is the configuration called *Komhrem*, comprising of five tribes of Manipur, namely Kom, Chiru, Aimol, Koren and Purum, which had made itself visible by way of cultural resemblance. This coming together of all such tribes is propelled by their exclusion from dominant tribal formations such as Hmar and Kuki. A culturally positive assertion against a perceived sense of marginalisation from the exterior creates resistance against cultural exclusion and cultural dominance. In their search for distinctness, the Hmars in Mizoram had created a narrative of cultural difference from Kukis and Mizos by referring to their distinct history and cultural memory.

The clash between Nagas and Kukis brings into focus the contest over territory and a kind of unreconciled sense of victim consciousness that turns into revenge in their drive for getting justice. Both Nagas and Kukis churn their memory in order to situate the events of brutalities and without being able to reconcile, it falls into the trap of violence-counter violence. What State aims at in such situations of clash is to settle its score against certain communities that question its authority and enforce peace through its penal apparatuses. This is how the State reacts to violence in civic sphere, stemming out of the conflict in native sphere. In its avowed objective of maintaining law and order, the State intervenes to discipline the warring communities and capitalises the sense of loss to forge some sort of reconciliation. This reconciliation remains as a loose embrace between them that loosens in the slightest fizz.

The role of an interventionist State in neutralising and quietening the clamours of identity that voice counterposing rights for itself, goes beyond civic statist-nationalist limits. It sponsors a kind of nationalism that suits well with the dominance created by the State. The Accords signed by the Indian State during eighties with AASU, TNV or MNF were all intended to strike a reconciliation with conflicting identities in order to subsume them under the State This will of the State presents a figure of dominance through its game of power that seeks to normalise the cultural politics of identities from below. The normalisation takes place by co-optation of advanced section of these identities into the fold of the State and this is how dominance re-enacts itself against resistance from below. What remains unrealisable under dominance is the independent and sovereign status of various identities, clamouring for their community aspirations. The State sponsored nationhood thrust from above dominates over the claims of nationhood from the communities below. As a result, the radical State supplants a kind of accommodation for these claimants, while radical nationality movements incorporate a demand for secession from the Indian State. The NSCN (I-M) demand for sovereignty, the ULFA demand for an independent Assam are all but a manifestation of reaction to the Statist approach to the nationality question and their struggle to sustain the emergence from below gives rise to 'nations from below' posed against a State-Nation that imposes a nationhood from above by way of granting subsidiary position to ethnic and cultural self-definitions.

III

But the crucial question that arises in any such emergence from below is that 'whether a coherentist Indian State-nation can allow a transgression of defined limits of statist sphere of politics without any coercion'. Streamlining and cohering smaller identities into a larger whole constitutes the Statist agenda of national integration, while smaller identities as actors in the sphere of state politics reproduce themselves in their distinctness. Democratization as part of statist agenda merely means the possibility of tying together such distinctive identities, while it excludes the possibility of contestation between such identities. As democratization through a process of contestation between identities assumes a greater possibility of a critique of statist politics, it is often disbanded by the State. Contestation as an inevitable consequence of reproduction of smaller identities on the stage of the State is encountered with a strategy of containment that shifts the balance of power towards the dominance of larger coherentist identities.

'Nations from below' is a metaphor for emergence of smaller identities by a contest with immediately dominant identity 'wholes', by an appropriation of its politics of coherence and homogeneity. The case of Bodo emergence marks such a contest against the dominance of Assamese nation and a elash with other peripheral and dominant identities such as Santhals, Bengalis, Koch etc. While the contest necessarily flows out of an appropriation of the dominant, the clash emanates out of refusal to tolerate other non-dominant identities. 'Nations from below' based upon socially rooted dominance acts *i.e.* smaller identities, which do not appropriate each other in the manner the dominant identities do. This cultivated politics of difference on the part of the dominant results in the clash of identities that sets aside issues of contestation. The clash between Bodos and Santhals brings forth the issue of 'who came first' or 'who is an encroacher' only to negatively strengthen the cultivated 'politics of difference' while refusing to appropriate each other's cultural and political positions. There is no contest over jobs, property, land, etc., but a question of setting 'who is first' which is a relapse into a primordialist position. Such clashes therefore, produce losses on both sides of Bodos and Santhals without a contest over definite 'areas of interests'. Further, absence of cultural appropriation between Bodos and Santhals spill over onto issues of ethnic, racial and religious differences creating fixations of paranoid kind, an ethno-pathology.

Such an ethno-pathology is the most dishevelling failure of statist politics of culture that embroils 'nations from below' into incoherent behavioural responses. The incoherence consists in repeatedly turning to instances of violation of community interests by others to turn the community against others in the immediate relationship. Ethno-pathology is that state of response in which others are perceived to be the source of diremption of one's own community, against which an emergence becomes necessary. The emergence is of the nature of an oppositional stemming out, which is un-mediated. It is the assumption of an agony of self-empowerment over others. Looked from another way, it is a way of defining others that detriments the community interests. One case in point is the definition of 'immigrant Bengali Muslims' who were perceived as potent imbalancing factor of demography, land, and community resources and a discourse of exclusion emanates from such an imposing definition. An ethno-pathological sensitivity perceives the other in fearful terms that analogise immigrant Muslim community as an UFO community. Such as analogy lightens up an omnipresence of immigrant Muslims and the ensuing danger from it. Such a construction of enemy conditions an emergence against them and puts them on the other side. This ethno-pathological construction of an enemy assumes a position of dominance up to a community and the victim turns into a subaltern from its excluded position. The resistance of victimised communities like Santhals, Bengalis, Kochs against such exclusion by the Bodos goes into re-defining themselves as legitimate settlers of the place. The wrath of Bodos upon them as a majority community fixes them as subalterns, as they are treated as outsiders in the Bodo areas. Again, within Bodos, the separation of Dimasas as a separate identity marks an emergence from the inclusivity ascribed to them.

'Nations from below' figures an articulation from an excluded position in order to recuperate the selflost in alien definitions. For immigrant Bengali Muslims of Char areas of Lower Assam, the experience of statist domination marking the dominance of dominant communities produced a loss of self-definition. Their experience of being washed away in floods, rampant governmental corruption and complete neglect from various agencies of development make them speak without an organisation that can represent them. They remain as an inarticulate community known at large as migrants from Bangladesh. The Santhal, Koch and many such ethnic communities of NE India who began to affirm themselves through their native organisation present a case for themselves and articulate a position of difference from the dominant. The contrast between such 'inarticulate' and 'articulate' communities looms large when inarticulate communities get defined in terms given by dominant others, while an 'articulate' community evolves a politically correct discourse about itself. An inarticulate community excluded from/by dominant identity is largely known by specific community markers neutralised and abstracted from the life-world of the community. For example, immigrant Bengali Muslims, Santhals and other smaller tribal communities like Mishing, Moran etc., are defined as 'immigrant', 'tribals' or 'labourers', in connotatives of 'lower' social positions. Such labels given on to them are categories of domination that enforces a simultaneous inclusion as being dominated and lost in greater articulated identities and exclusion from these legitimately constituted spaces because of their self-identity. Knowing Bengali Muslims as 'immigrants' or 'foreigners' or as people living in river islands inscribe at literally excluded location with a metaphorically lost sense of identity. The politics of dominations revolves around assignment of a place or value within articulated space of culture. An exclusion of Hmars, Brus or Chakmas from the articulated cultural and political space of Mizos or an exclusion of Muslims and smaller tribal communities from an articulated space of Assamese identity simultaneously represent their exclusion from the dominant and their appropriation within the dominant. The exclusion signifies the arrogance of the dominant from yielding a democratic space to these communities and their appropriation commands them to follow a legitimate and legitimised path of politics and culture. Exclusion further signifies the possibility of emergence of small identities as a distinct identity and political appropriation signifies a norm governed situation within legitimate forms of dominant politics.

The inarticulate identities are made the subject of State discourses, such as development of Char areas, or improvement of conditions of peasant folk. The State always situates these identities in an excluded space and marks them as the subject of discourse. Statist discourses then go for elimination of such excluded identities as 'references' and the exclusion is complete when they are categorised in quantitative and objective terms. Therefore, one can say that the state assumes the agency for structuring such identities into some translatable, rational and development oriented messages or public 'packages' meant for them which are diversified to accommodate 'all' into a conglomerate nation space. Such a conglomerate space is marked by mechanical reproduction of social identities and it tends to encode them in terms of statist quota and norms. For example, statist definition of scheduled tribe in India or more specifically an agency like North Eastern Council aiming to perpetuate the idea of a 'region', almost of colonial type safeguards the dependency relationship between Indian state and the region called 'North East'.

This structuration of identities by the State has two levels of discursive production, at one level, identities are aroused to organise resistance to their structuration from their position as 'other' and at another level, a contra-state 'other' levels of discursive production, social identities explore alternate position, an articulation of which is simultaneously ethno-centric and resistant to the state. Also within ethno-centricity, a weak response to the other makes it feebly selfish, while a stronger and articulate response to the other produces a sense of fidelity to the ways in which the self evolves in the community. Resistance remains as the prime motivating force for a community to turn inward and ethno-centric.

IV

This resistance takes a metaphoric name with a metaphoric meaning from the Indian State. 'Insurgency', as it is called, signifies a subversion of the Statist strategies and policies of dominance. In the sphere of culture, it means a rejection of the 'national' in favour of the 'native', a celebration of the indigenous and ethnic over the civic popular culture. In the case of NE India, greater acceptance of western popular and media culture is also subversive of the dominant Hindi-Hindu national culture, which at the same time means consumption of modern culture with their own ethnic mode of life.

Insurgency establishes a naturalised affinity of the mass with those media images that present triumph of masculine and macho forces over media, systemic and governmental agencies. It induces a regime of supermen, gangsters, terrorists, spy and spy catcher flowing from Amercanised industries of film and media. [4] The instant popularity of such images perpetuates the already seething discontent with the non-indigenous populace and the Indian State. The cultural resistance also assumes a guerrilla war image against dominant cultural figures having its ready homology with urban guerrilla figures in the media.

What this pattern of cultural preference indicates is a sharp distinction drawn between one's own cultural roots and dominant cultural images. In ethnic terms, this distinction is actualised by clearly demarcating the cultural boundary of an ethnic group from others. This is demonstrated in the distinctions that exist between self-enclosed ethnic communities from 'others'. One can observe examples such as how smaller communities such as 'Paite', Baite', 'Phom' etc. distinguished themselves from their brethren communities like Hmar, Lushei and Kuki and claim themselves as separate tribes. Similarly distinctions of a generic inter-tribal nature such as sense of difference existing between Khasis and Mizos present a picture of ethnic consciousness that assumes the content of nationhood in spirit. The consciousness is based upon drawing a distinction between 'inside' and 'outside' while the 'inside' fashions itself in relation to the 'outside'. The positioning of the self and the community requires an 'inside' to sustain its identity by way of counter position to the process of abstraction of generic markers out of their localised existence. This 'positioning' is very relevant in grasping the resistance to dominance, as it operates as a network of power that fixes dominance of an identity to a definite position within the network. 'State', acting as an 'outside' with its national network of power forces a community of North East India to position itself inside the network by way of distinguishing itself from an 'outside' and this is how community places itself in the signifiers of domination and sees itself different from others. In the context of cultural reproduction of the community, the ethnic signified plays the role of retaining a mark of self-identify and difference simultaneously without merging itself with a generalised reproduction of the Nation. Often it clashes with the dominant 'others' without diluting its self-identity. [5]

This positioning of the self in various indigenous communities takes a metaphoric meaning in designating the 'outside'. In the context of NE India, the metaphor 'outsider' assumes a crucial importance in relating itself to the State. 'Outsider' becomes the code for settling scores with other communities in which the State is dragged in addressing the unfulfilled aspirations of a community. Often 'outsider' becomes synonym for identifying an alien State machinery in tandem with business establishment, all of which stand together in depriving the NE region from many essential developments. The coding of 'outsider' on the issues of granting citizenship to Chakmas, Nepalis, Bengalis, acts as a legal camouflage to manouver the State and reclaim the indigenous authority. The conflict over citizenship figures out the greater claim of indigenous rights over universalising and expanding field of citizen rights, levelling everyone on the same footing. 'Outsider' encodes the apprehension of the native communities on the unreserved extension of citizenship rights in the ethnic habitats of NE India producing many encroachments. The sense of being an 'Indian' is constructed by the citizenship acquired from the 'State' to enter into the ethnic domain of communities in the most intriguing ways. Metaphor of 'outsider' situates the peculiar position of the ethnic communities in the midst of an ever widening field of citizenry and conversely the citizenship that cannot but make an inroad into the ethnic domain to make it equal with others in every respect. 'Outsider' as a metaphor signifies the internalisation of citizenship among the ethnic communities of NE India. Figuring an outsider further signifies occupation of a space within the space of Nation.

V

Resistance of the ethnic communities of NE India expresses itself into something legitimate from the perspective of the State [6]. This legitimate camouflage is utilised in demanding certain rights that have been hitherto denied to a community of the NE India. Through such encoding of legitimate rights, the communities articulate their sovereignty. For example, the demand of Bodoland Autonomous Council for inclusion of many villages of controversial kind in the proposed 'Bodoland' shows the legal battle that a surging ethnic group can fight with the State. This kind of legitimate demands often occasion a tirade against others from extremist factions. The state aims at resolving such demands through both deliberative and coercive means. The legitimate demands of an ethnic community gain legitimacy by way of questioning certain principles and acts of the State that supposedly go against the genuine rights and aspirations of the indigenous people. This critical legitimacy of the ethnic movements earns legitimacy in the consideration of the community which often questions the authority of the state in the sphere of norms. This requires an agenda of counter-legitimacy which is attained by way of rejection of norms and laws framed by the State and by way of affirming the specific ethnic standpoint. Such counter-affirmations often clash with inviolable essentials laid down by the state. The logic of insurgency is such that in distinguishing an inside from outside and in encoding its message in a legitimate demand it aims at subverting the essential of the State like 'sovereignty' and 'terriotoriality'. In the context of NE India, it occurs by way of affirmation of national rights and separate homeland for an ethnic community, which produces the condition of displacement of the ideological and ethnic basis of the state. It primarily counter-poses the concept of a unified civil society and unitary civic sphere of rights, which by implication induces an independent claim of national right with sovereignty unto an ethnic group. [7] The response of the State is counter-insurgency violence aimed at curbing the struggle of smaller ethnic groups.

VI

The consequence of this struggle between legitimacy and counter-legitimacy is the struggle between ethnic community and the State. The mobilisation of insurgency is counteracted by the State by way of de-recognising the claims of 'nation' from below. There have been allegations of atrocities and counter atrocities from both the battling sides. The cases of torture and atrocities produce a sense of warfare between the State and the communities. In case of NE India, the centre of the struggle remains a lasting and continuous process of violence and counter violence that takes turns to events of State sponsored atrocity as well as atrocities on ethnic minorities. The State attributes militant violence as 'terrorism', while it does not recognise the demand for recognition of ethnic communities in its operation for peace. One of the Amnesty International reports entitled, India 'Operation Bluebird': A Case Study of Torture and Extra judicial Executions in Manipur. (October, 1990) stated,[8]

> "The testimonies cited (.....) demonstrate that witnesses giving evidence in court face a real risk of repercussions. This is one of the reasons why victims have only rarely complained to the civilian courts, even though reports of human rights violation in the North East have been frequent. Another reason is that the victims live in inaccessible regions with poor communications, the only contact many have with outsiders is the Army. Many are illiterate, and they often do not know how to approach the courts, and do not have funds to bring legal action and believe that petitions would not be accepted. Although villagers have complained to the civilian authorities such as the local police or deputy commissioner, these authorities have often said that they felt powerless to do anything about matters concerning security forces that are controlled by the central government. Finally, (...) section 6 of the Armed Forces Special Powers Act prevents citizens from bringing a case against the security forces without prior permission from the central government."

Such 'subjects' of State violence heighten the already embedded structural lacks such as illiteracy, poverty, backwardness on the one hand and legal blockage on the other accentuating misrecognition of collective aspiration by the State and widening the base for collective struggle for redemption from State repression.[9]

The tendency of ethnic cleansing by targeting an ethnic minority is also a surrogate of this dominance of the State and surge for liberation of an ethnic community. The cases at Nelli, Kokrajhar in Assam, Bilonia in Tripura etc, present the misplaced anger of ethnic communities on minorities, who are neither properly protected by the State nor they are secure in their socio-economic position. The persecution of such minorities could be taken as a displacement of ethnic aspirations in annihilation of fellow human beings, who as settlers never enjoy privileges unattainable by an indigenous community. The ethnicized arena of struggle benumbs the emergence of national aspirations from below, when the struggle turns on curbing other communities from the most basic aspiration of life.

VII

Is there a way to redescribe this whole situation? One can notice the reactivity against dominance in NE India expressed in terms of encroachment of a community's rights and also in terms of blaming other communities *vis-a-vis* the State. In all its expressions, it assumes a subaltern position in articulating a position of difference and subordination. From this position of difference and subordinatian the primary target remains the State, while a different cultural group and its dominant image produces a reaction at the secondary level. This assumption of a subaltern position by an ethnic group takes place in a terrain of struggle to resist its inclusion within a generic 'national' configuration by the State. The struggle brings out an 'alterity', a 'different' position by a political interpretation given onto an 'other'. These two simultaneous struggles to resist totalisation within 'nation' and an affirmation of difference by creating an inside inverts the dominant discourse. The cultural devaluation of an ethnic community from within the dominant nationalist culture compounded with the strategy of subordinating it to a civic Statist sphere releases a string of counter responses that articulate this experience of asymmetry in politics. This inversion of the dominant discourse prioritises 'nation from below' as possible altern positions that are subordinated from a position of 'nation from above'. The 'nation from below' expresses itself not through the State conduits but by striking against an established harmony by way of extreme means. What is important here is to note that the affirmation of a subaltern ethnic group negates the State and designs an expression for itself in order to make it visible. It seems, that the selective struggle with the State, claim of national identity by an ethnic community and its politics of difference have to be filled with events of violence.

VIII

Violence plays an important role in instilling ethnic markers in terms of difference. But a politics of difference puts into play the limits of the already evolved and legitimised social identities to generate contest over those already settled markers and norms. Within the nation-space, the primacy of certain stable and legitimate markers produces a sense of certitude in accepting certain larger and common identity as self-definition. Such a primacy is throttled when the limits of various community and ethnic self-definition are played in its distinctness. This further signifies an alteration of the dominant and central imagination of nation in a discursive way. Certain other discursively neglected and inarticulate forms of identities could well be special cases for reconsidering already beset boundaries of various communities.

This whole process signifies the possibilities of violation or violability of so far sacrosanct national self-definition and a way of overcoming strictly defined identities by certain interpretation and re-interpretation of their boundaries. A definite amount of sensitisation accompanies this process of reconfiguration of ethnic boundaries. The felicity of being reconsidered as a distinct entity through a performative reappropriation and demonstration of one's own heritage is like recasting / re-embodying oneself with a gesture of identity, something new and yet so passionately drawn from 'a certain source of collective identification'. Within the nation-space, such an emergence means tangible redrawing of physical and political boundaries, with which the State should come to terms.[11] The coming to terms of the State flags off a politics of consolidation in echelons of power by various identities. This becomes a moment of internal and external contest for various identities. But what the State peremptorily does is to stabilise the fuzziness of ethnic and cultural boundaries, that is, fuse them into categories of power/authority. This logic of the State runs counter to the logic of identity politics. For a State like the Indian State, accommodation of emergent identities by the State is directed to strengthen and widen the space of national identity. State reinforces a national identity over contesting identities without addressing the issues of contestation. Indian State designs a politics of piece meal redressal for singular communities [12] that increase separatist tendencies.

Indian State projects the dominant identity as the only legitimate identity that can resolve contestation between identities. We can call it identity-given-by-the-State. An identity contesting such a given identity by invoking culture-specific sense of identity contests the State. The State could be contested by such identities because of its partial and preferential inclination to some dominant identities having its influence upon the State, interests of which are protected under the universalist identity-given-by-the State. State, in fact, gets identified with such dominant social identities and it can no longer protect the interests of smaller identities. Therefore, smaller identities need to negotiate from a position of 'subaltern' as imposed on them by the State.

The identity-given-by-the-State and the State-sponsored dominant identity de-recognise the specific cultural claims of other smaller identities. This leads to their subordination and subjugation within the 'dominant', which means that there is a constant encoding of their culturally specific mores within the dominant, which disorients them from the means of articulation. Being culturally and politically situated as subjugated, they are forced to articulate in the language of the dominant and thereby displace their own cultural reference in terms of the dominant. This experience of acculturation is induced by State-sponsored dominant identity and more inflictingly by the imposing national identity given by the State.

There is another way of operation of the dominant by way of exclusion of its 'others' as different. 'Others' are delegitimised even though they are recognised as 'others'. This delegitimsation of 'others' from the 'dominant' who holds its influence over the State neutralises it from protecting them. Such delegitimised identities are forced to articulate a case from a marginalised and excluded position. The dominant discourse that pushes them outside the legitimised sphere of culture and politics is contested by these delegitimised identities from an excluded subaltern position. Their position of being excluded creates a space for interrogating the legitimised, identities, its exclusivism by expressing self-determination.

The role of the Indian State in enforcing a national identity by means of dominance and subaltern heightens the rationale of forming the centralized national identity dominant in character. The dominant identities created by the Indian State cobble together as the markers of a unified, singular State community and fuse it into a well formed entity. Such markers are chosen selectively in order to reduce distinctiveness of various segments within a community and give it a common colour. This process of muting of identities by the rationale of domination from the State makes it a State Nation or 'Nation from above'.

IX

In the context of North-East India, creation of identity-given-by-the-State in terms of recognition and legitimation got directly intertwined with dominant identity formations. Even though such formations contested the dominant national identity their recognition by the State strengthened and widened the space of national identity. The naming of an Assamese identity and acceptance of its demands by the Indian State, which is a result of six-years long Assam Movement, strengthened both the Indian national identity as well as appropriation of smaller identities within a conglomerate Assamese identity. In the case of a State like Tripura, recognition of tribal and non-tribal identities by the Indian State is a continuation of the same process of strengthening national identity as well as the dominant identity.

But such State-sponsored dominant identities involve a picture of contestation. Cases like Assamese, Mizo and Naga identities refusing to be included within Indian identity are still contesting cases. Therefore, the successful and unsuccessful attempts of the Indian State to incorporate such identities within a conglomerate national identity remained a mere statist appropriation, while the identities resisted such appropriation tactics. Therefore, Statist appropriation merely produced State national identities, while distinct national identities of such communities remained as nations from below. Below the level at which Indian State circumscribed these identities within a dominant national form they retained a distinct indigenous form of their own. In other words, State enforced a lowering of indigenous inscription of such identities.

X

Against the appropriation by the State of various social identities in the network of nationalising them, various such identities register their emergence. The claim of United Liberation Front of Assam in asserting that Assamese nationality is formed by a historically specific process of common nationality struggle participated by various smaller communities of Assam set aside the project of Statist-Nationalist historical claim of anti-colonial struggle. ULFA delineates a different process of mobilisation of various sections of masses during anti-British struggle and read it as different from the nationalist angle. This distinction from a shared pan-Indian hisotry empowers the Assamese nation to assert itself against statist appropriation from above. In case of Naga assertion a similar politics of statist appropriation is countered and resisted. Nagas strike a different note against statist appropriation. V.S. Atem, the chief of NSCN(I-M)'s arms wing aptly states.[13]

> .... Yes, no one would like to fight. But since this is a matter of right, we take it as good as our own life, so it is the question of life and death, so whether we like to fight or not, we are compelled to fight.

General Atem is speaking here of a perennial imperative to fight against appropriation by the Indian State. This is an emergence against the Statist- Nationlist formation of Naga identity, an identity that fits well with the normative order of the state.

In the context of Naga struggle, the experience of being dispersed in many states occupation of Southern part of Nagaland by India, Indo-Myanmar's joint offensive against the Nagas are referred by Naga leaders as examples of systematic statist appropriation. From these experiences, the struggle derives its political content of unification of Naga territory to spread across national and transnational areas. The possibility of achieving a unified Naga homeland produces a counter-discourse to the statist discourse of redressal of grievances and its settlement within the frame of Indian Constitution. The discourse of Naga nationalism undercuts the statist division of Naga territories as well as manoeuvering of this division by wielding the spectre of pan-Indian nationalism.

In case of Mizo struggle, it originated from the failure of the Indian State to control famine in Mizoram. Interrogation of the scope of democratic procedures of the Indian State by the Mizos opened up the history of independence of Mizos from Indian rule since the British days and exposed the political illegitimacy of Indian hegemony over Mizos during post-1947 period. The signing of the Mizo Accord in 1985 marked in a sense the end of the struggle.

In all such cases, the feature of appropriation of an ethnic community by the Indian State through formation of a defined identity was contested by affirming ethnically specific ways of life by identities like Assamese, Naga and Mizo. The need for affirmation arose from contesting the culturally dominant identity that came to be imposed upon them through a statist mechanism. The statist concept of Indian nationhood did not have any legitimate grounding within these communities except wielding of State power. The percolation of influence of other dominant ethnic communities in the civic sphere also became a contestable terrain for native communities. So, there was a three-fold mediation from above by the State :

(i) construction of a defined ethnic identity 'in' and 'through' State power,
(ii) legitimising such a State-defined identity by including it within an Indian identity, and
(iii) percolating dominance of other communities in the ethnic sphere.

All these three mediatory moves by the Indian State came from above, as none of these could grow from within. These produced a spectre of domination upon the native haunting them by the apprehension of being submerged by other dominated communities. This created an effect of being dominated and disempowered among various native communities of NE India. Correspondingly, they responded by way of contesting the mechanism and the effect of such a statist-nationalist process from above. The attempt of the state to construct a defined identity was contested by constructing a self-definition with a greater latitude. Especially the concept of 'nationalism' in case of various NE India communities assumed a sovereign and independent homeland, undercutting the threads of Indian statist-nationalist definition. So far as legitimation of such well-defined identities within the State was concerned the identities interrogated the legitimacy of the Indian State itself. Further, they questioned the formation and structuration of their community within an arbitrary political unit through their own political bodies. The dominance of others in the civic sphere became immediate bone of contention for all such communities. In all these counter-political moves by ethnic identities the Indian State became the object of critique/critic, centering which ethnic movements asserted from below and attempted at emancipating them through their counter-discourses.

But the construction of 'nations from below' produced an autonomous sphere of dominance that got enmeshed with the statist mechanisms from above. The case of Bodo uprising against the dominance of Assamese community from within, the case of Hmars from within Mizos etc. portray that dominance of particular section of the unified identity produces resistance from within. The politics of statist appropriation extends through dominance of the elites within an identity against which its own internal others fight. The Bodos, Kochs, tribals like Mishing, Miri etc. within Assamese identity found themselves unrepresented and neglected. Similar is the case with Hmars of Mizoram.

Here we have to make a distinction between cases of Bodos or Hmars with the cases of those who are excluded and delegitimised in the process of constructing the dominant identity. The case of Santhals, Bengali Muslims, Chakmas, Brus are some of the cases. These communities were treated by the contiguous native communities as refugees or migrants. They became the subjects of ethnic violence precisely because the dominant communities intended to register the strength of their movement by ostracising and cleansing them. These subjects of violence were made defenceless victims as the legitimacy of their existence was debunked by the dominant communities. Discussion of certain paradoxes is illuminating here.

In the context of Bodo movement, the rage against the Santhals was paradoxical as Bodos as an ethnic minority were fighting against Assamese hegemony. The question is how can they riot against the Santhals, who are another ethnic minority? The logic of violence could be explained in terms of displaced anger. The subjects of such displaced anger are the 'new subalterns' who did not even have a language to articulate their pain.

The Bengali Muslims similarly are 'soft targets' of ethnicised 'displaced anger'. One can explain it in terms of a revenge motive against the State and dominant community, who is seen as the cause of presence of 'others' in one's own land. A kind of 'Lebenseraum' motif of cleansing the space from communities who are different operates in the action-programme of ethnic organisations.

The rage against Brus or Chakmas is also a product of a supposedly incommensurable presence of these communities in someone else's home. The case of expatriation of large number of Brus from Mizoram or Paites from Manipur presents a picture of an increasingly hostile inter-ethnic co-existence.

A State-nation never allows various ethnic formations to grow independently in their own ethics and so it constantly interrupts them from various sources such as economy and politics producing a terrain of clash between communities. When issues become troubles, contestation over symbols, myths and authority remains unresolved within the parameters of civil society and so the State takes this clashing turn. The State, once again, comes down heavily from above to clear out the whole terrain of contest, resulting in many an inter-ethnic clashes and blatant human rights violations.

NOTES AND REFERENCES

* The term 'new Subaltern' as different from 'Subaltern' not only refers to identities produced from their dominated positions but a description of the graver feature of benumbing their expression of pain by way of complete and rapacious violence on them. This also gives birth to 'rebel consciousness'. This term has been discussed extensively, perhaps for the first time by Prof. Gayatri Spivak at the VIth Subaltern Studies Conference in 1998.

1. Verrier Flwin. *A Philosophy for North East Frontier Agency*. Shillong. 1959 p. 145.
2. Customary rights specify places of significance by custom for ethnic communities of NE India. It also specifies conventions by which such rights are endowed.
3. Sanjoy St. *Strangers of the Mist : Tales of War and Peace from India's North East*, Penguin, 1994, p.c354. He cites example of an Assamese teacher who instructs students to sing Assamese National Anthem instead of National Anthem.
4. Various pulp fiction written in vernacular such as Mizo, Khasi etc, are already available along with high demand of various films and images from the West .
5. P.S. Dutta (ed.) *Ethnic Movements in Poly-Cultural Assam*, Vikas, New Delhi, 1990, p. 19 He gives an example where Dutta commented:

    'We are yet to have a definition of Asamese which is stable over time and place and people. With the changing circumstances the definition too changes. On some people an Asssames identity is imposed while some others are allowed to accept an Assamese identity. At another point of time the allured neo-Assamese are identified as non-Assamese and hence non-Indian.'

One can read here how self-identity is never diluted, but constantly rehashed as a process of struggling against 'others'.

6. Insurgency encodes itself within something legitimate as strategy.
7. The demand for sovereignty is a common theme among most of the eminent nationalist groups from NE India.
8. Sanjoy Hazarika *op. cit.*, p. 373.
9. This kind of struggle against State repression mobilises democratic section of the masses and also puts the State at a receiving end by bringing into light the atrocities committed by the State.
10. Marion O' Callaghan. "Continuities of Imagination" in N.Pieterse *et. al.* (ed) *The Decolonization of Imagination: Culture, Knowledge, Power*, OUP, Delhi, 1995.
11. One can refer to demands like Bodoland, unification of Naga inhabited areas etc.
12. Various Accords such as Mizo Accord , Assam Accord etc. have taken care of demands of the dominant communities. In case of Mizo Accord, the demands for Hmar Autonomous Council was not incorporated . In Assam Accord, linguistic and religious minorities of the State were given a fair deal. The Accords remained ethno-centric and exclusive in character.
13. Interview with V.S. Atem. In *New -Sun*, March 1-14, 1998, p.9.
14. How such violations of human rights are taking place is evident from the mass scale death due to non-supply of succour to the camps inhabited by victims of riots. The total number of such riot-refugees reached a few lakhs. There has been rampant child mortality, sickness and death prevalent in such camps. There are cases when camp dwellers have been attacked by killer gangs during day and night time. One can refer to *Sadin*, Vol. X, No. 18, 17th July, 1998. p.1 and p.22 for a deft reporting of such events.

12

Human Rights and Nationalised Civilisations

B. S. Butola

Generalised alienation and universalised estrangement is ontological to capitalism. Extended commodity reproduction under capitalism includes the commodification of human beings, meaning thereby that dehumanisation is the process of capital accumulation, which in turn is the basis of Capitalism. The essence of this system lies in generalised commodity production where, the worker not only produces the commodities but, produces himself as a commodity, subjected to the laws of market *i.e.* to be purchased and sold in the market. Thus, the product of his own labour confronts the worker something as alien. The product gains its objectification and recognition with the worker, the producer, experiencing loss of this realisation. He is governed by the objective world of the products he produces. The forces of this alien world not only separate the producer from the product but it also estranges him from himself, his fellow beings and the nature and the organic links with it. Isolation of individuals and erosion of ones creativity reduces the worker to atomised existence devoid of any transcendental potential. Socialisation of material world and atomisation of the individuals completely isolates the individual and superficial communications fail to articulate the depth of the inner world particularly its internal contradiction and conflicts. That is the reason why it fails to break the loneliness in an absurd world. As a result, the humans feel themselves free only in animal functions like eating, drinking, procreating in dressing-up or at most feeling free in his dwelling etc., but in his human functions he no longer feels himself to be anything but an animal. " What is animal becomes human and what is human becomes animal."[1] Apart from the loss of essence, purpose and realisation in life , exploitation, accumulation, and greed of exchange value are the absolute laws of capitalism. So long such a system continues it will be always detrimental to human freedom including civil and human rights. According to Albert Camus " choosing freedom is not as we are told choosing against justice. On the other hand, freedom is chosen today in relation to those who are everywhere suffering and fighting, and this is the only freedom that counts. It is chosen at the same time as justice and to tell the truth henceforth, we cannot have one without the other. If some one takes away your bread he suppresses your freedom at the same time. But if someone takes away your freedom you may be sure that your bread is threatened, for it no longer depends on you and your struggle but on the whims of a master. Poverty increases in so far as freedom retreats throughout the world and vice versa"[2]. It means freedom, civil rights, human rights etc., are antithetical to capitalism. This is perhaps the bitter truth that the protagonists of liberal democracy will find difficult to digest.

Based on the assumption that the very existence of this inhuman system makes the realisation of all kinds of freedom and rights difficult and impossible, in this article an attempt has been made to evaluate the possibilities of realisation of human rights in relation to one of the most distinguished feature of the modern world system *i.e.* the Nation.

Interrogating the Nation

The four pillars of the modern world are Enlightenment, Rationality, Modernity and Nation. Of these, Nation is of paramount importance for representing the epitome of a dialectical unity of freedom and subjugation, emancipation and exploitation of human beings, emanating from one and the same historical process. The history of the modern world system presents a unique synthesis of such contradictions. Freedom in one country/region is possible by dominating the other subjects, territories and claims. Therefore, though Nation as a socio-historical entity is of a very recent origin yet, it has occupied a central position in most of the contemporary discourses. According to most of the scholars, the process of Nation formation started initially in Europe during 18th and 19th centuries and thereafter, it spread all over the world. It is mainly for this special feature that Walter Bagehot named this epoch as the "Century of Nation Building"[3]. To be more precise E.J. Hobsbawm identified this period as between 1780 and 1880 AD. He emphasised that this period was dominated by the understanding of the term Nation and the vocabulary from it[4]. It is remarkable to know that within such a short span of time Nation has gained the dimensions of permanence and universality. It has become so pervasive that it even dominates the human imagination and shapes their dreams. Nation as a totality ensembling national language, religion, culture, spirit, ethos and ethics has evolved into an autonomous entity. And for all these years Nation stood for 'Something' and all the other entities were relegated merely to the 'Other' of this over-arching and universalising entity. Nation has become the ultimate in the evolution of humans as social, political, cultural and economic beings. It has also become the apex in the evolution of identity and spatial/ geographical formations. Subsequently, evolution and culmination of the 'Others' into Nation is not only considered normal but inevitable and necessary too. Today, this process is universally accepted almost like the law of gravity and every 'Other' is considered as a deviation or aberration from the norm and therefore, deserves secular denigration and condemnation. Thus, evolution of smaller cultures communities and identities into the larger national identity has not only become a passion for the smaller, marginal and subaltern identities but it has also become the sole justifying rational process in the saga of human evolution. This has also become the unitary aspiration of every different identity group for seeking the twin justices of redistribution and recognition. Corresponding to these changes, various discourses were constructed around this particular gravitational pull.

The period after the World War II has special significance in the history of nation formation world over. This period was marked by its own laws and contradictions. It witnessed an epoch of juxtapositions of national liberation and subjugation, of emergence and breaking up of nations, of wars and peace between the nations etc. As a consequence of this the national space changed so much within so little time that for many it was the beginning of the end of a prolonged honeymoon for the Nation. The emergence of nations after the War, largely due to sustained freedom struggles and national liberation movements mostly fought against the European colonisers provided great encouragement to other subjugated and marginalised nationalities. Moreover, the recognition of the civil rights and human rights over and above the national rights have further contributed to the crises of the Nation. But, of all the challenges and crises faced by the Nation so far, crises which emerged after 1960s are of special significance. The challenges are so widespread and genuine that it has shaken the very foundation of Nation as an institution . And what is more surprising to notice is that there is no alternative to it. The situation is far more grave in a Nation like India that emerged after the World War II.

Crisis of the Nation-State : The Nemesis

According to Istvan Hont the term Crisis is a medical metaphor depicting the decisive moment when a patient's fate is sealed[5]. Crisis here means a clear deterioration in the capacity of the nation-state to master the hazards to the security and prosperity of its subjects[6]. In politics it simply means the acknowledgement of some degree of real challenge to the existing routines such that it may no longer be possible in Lenin's lapidary phrase "to go on in its old way"[7]. In the contemporary situations this particular task before the nation-state of looking after the welfare of its citizens has become difficult mainly because of the following reasons:

The first and foremost important challenge posed before the Nation is the forces of global economic liberalisation[8]. It has become the common experience of all the Nation-States that their power to take care of their subject has correspondingly decreased with the increase in the forces of globalisation of the world economy. The process of economic liberalisation has proved detrimental to the Keynesian concept of Welfare State particularly in taking full responsibility for the economic welfare of its subjects. Thus, the concept of a genuine Welfare State is increasingly becoming a nightmare to the contemporary Nation-States. Under the new global economic system it has become imperative to all the trading partners of the multilateral trade to cut down and ultimately do away with their welfare measures including subsidies provided by the State in various spheres of economy. The threat to the sovereignty of the Nation-State has come essentially from the tension between a national framework of sovereign authority and governmental responsibility and an uncompromisingly international field of economic causality[9].

The other formidable challenge has been posed by the increasing environmental degradation[10]. In the sphere of ecology too, the Nation-States have come under tension. It is mainly due to the fact that the ecological degradation like global warming, acid rain, depletion of the ozone layer, emission of green house gases etc., have no national boundary and it affects the quality of life of every citizen irrespective of their nationalities. The Nation-States are not in a position to do any thing to improve the fast deteriorating situation. Thus, failure on the part of the Nation-States to control the ecological degradation on the hand and failure in assuring safe future to its citizens on the other, has also undermined the capacity of these institutions.

Yet another formidable challenge has come from the new class of its citizens that have resulted from the large-scale transnational migrations[11]. Migration in the contemporary times is qualitatively different from the one that existed in the past. Today, more people than ever before seem to routinely imagine the possibility that they or their children will live and work in places other than where they were born. This is not a simple aspiration of the contemporary generations but it is more fundamental than this. It has given rise to new social ethos, project and mythographies[12]. As a result of this, nations are over populated by the people with no culture of their own and no roots to stand on. Nations are increasingly being peopled by people who are not only rootless but live in a cultural vacuum and emotional void without any commitment to any thing that can match with national ethos, heritage and ethics.

The other challenge is from the field of technology and technocratisation of culture. Use of mass electronic media in promoting the corporate culture and mass cultural images and symbols have created the possibilities of collective imaginings that have more powerful and far reaching consequence than the imaginative boundaries of a nation. In a nutshell, the combination of electronic mediation and mass migration has created the new diasporic public spheres that transcend the boundaries of Nation-State[13].

Yet another important challenge comes from the upsurge of the ethnic and identity movements world over. The rise of the so-called ethnic nationalist movements indicating the crises of the nation is largely regulated through the forces of global multi-national capitalism. A sovereign Nation is increasingly proving the most fundamental obstacle in the promotion of these forces. For overthrowing the Nation-States from within the multi-national capitalist interests are actively engaged in the subversion of the Nation from within, and interestingly without provoking the nationalist sentiments against the aggressor[14] .

Last but in no way least important challenge to the Nation comes from the inherent contradictions that are ensembled within the concept " Nation". In the age of falling paradigms particularly after the recognition of identity, politics and ideology of difference, the inhuman and illegitimate facets of the Nation have made it vulnerable to criticism. Nation everywhere, stands interrogated for coercion, domination and overtly naked display of power and covertly an apex institution of surveillance and constant vigilance. The way the Nation uses and exploits the capillary powers for dehumanising the human beings, for suppressing of the human freedom has led to violation of Human Rights. The history of modern nations is nothing but the emergence, expansion and consolidation of apparatuses of administrative intervention in and control over the social world with Pastoral Power[15]. This new dimension of power works more on mind rather than on the body and so the citizens are under perpetual moral and psychological imprisonment. The ultimate stage is the violation of human rights.

Thus, the crises of the Nation have multiplied greatly and their magnitude and dimensions have also become insurmountable to any Nation-State. The crises are so deep and have such far and wide ramifications that the nationalist discourses developed around the Nation are also being interrogated from various quarters and positions. Along with this, the postulations of modernity and the Enlightenment movements are also being refuted mostly by the Post-Nationalist, the Deconstructionist, the Post-modernist and the Post-Structuralist philosophers. At times the refutations are so genuine that these philosophies are increasingly becoming the rallying points for the dissolution of the Nations. Therefore, it is essential to critically evaluate the theoretical and philosophical promises of the Nation. It is so because nations are over and above a spatial, political, philosophical ideological, cultural, psychological and economic entities and crises in these get articulated not only in the disintegration of the nation but in the future of mankind in general. Therefore, it is essential to investigate into these postulations of the Nation that have been put under interrogation and posed crisis of integration.

Novelty and Banality of Nation

The concept Nation meant many things to many people till the end of seventeenth century. In earlier discourses on the United States of America scholars preferred to use the concept like 'the people', the confederation 'our common land' 'the public' 'the community' etc. in order to avoid the centralizing and unitary implications of the term Nation. It was only during the era of revolutions that the French used the term Nation "the one and the indivisible". It was only in the aftermath of the French and the American revolutions that it ventilated the literature that equated it with something political[16]. The "Nation so considered was the body of citizens whose collective sovereignty constituted them as a State, which was their political expression. For, whatever else a Nation was, the element of citizenship and mass participation or choice was never absent from it[17]. Sovereignty remained one of the inalienable characteristic features of it. Nation represented and symbolised the victory of common interest against particular interest, common good against the privilege of a few and it was not in any fundamental sense, ethnicity, language and the like[18]. But, unfortunately, the sublime foundations of the secular Nation were displaced in the subsequent phase and thereafter it started representing the common sentiments of one ethnic group against another, one language verses another, one religion verses another, one territory and heritage verses another. In fact, it is argued that the French Revolution was not only foreign to the principle or feelings of nationality but, it was also hostile to it. But, in the aftermath of this particular historic event, narrow and sectarian bases of nation have not only occupied the centre stage but it has also become the supreme virtue and indomitable spirit world over. Thus, nations that were based on the principle of tolerance and accommodation have become intolerant and hostile to each other. This has posed serious problems to the efforts of gaining and retaining one's freedom and rights. It is interesting to note that the sublime concept of Nation in the context of India in general and its North-Eastern parts in particular has got dittoed, as various Nationalist movements are not only based on the non-secular and parochial foundations but on the hostility against the other which provides the basis of their existence. These nationalist movements mostly thrive upon generating hatred against the other which is more fundamental to their existence than their faith in the ideology of human liberation and commitment to the general well being. The region witnesses suppression of civil and human rights both by the Indian State as well as the aspirants of separate Nationalities. The sublime is thus ridiculed.

Totality and the Totalitarian Nation

Defining Totality, Sartre postualted that it is a being which, while radically distinct from the sum of its parts, is present in its entirety, in one form or another, in each of these parts, and which relates to itself either through its relation to one or more of its parts or through its relation to the relation between all or some of them[19]. The entirety of a Nation lies in its evolution from ethnic, religious, racial, cultural and economic interest or identity formation into an over arching and an ensembling system of values, symbols, cultures, political system, sovereignty, national spirit, economic interest, political ideology, social philosophy and ultimately the political power. Once, one or a combination of a few of these identities succeed in grabbing the political power and subsequently in presenting a blue print of evolution before the other competing systems, it gains a synthesis of time and space, general and particular, and interiority and exteriorty. In doing so it not only severes all its previous connections and engages itself in distancing itself from the 'Other' which it denigrates now as primordial thus retrogressive but also thrives by negating, subjugating and if possible annihilation of the 'Other'. In order to maintain the vision of totality the Nation continuously strives for maintaining a dynamic balance between internal legalisation or consent and external autonomy or sovereignty by presenting itself as the true object of the all seeing eyes totally accessible and transparent. For achieving the ideological dominance the nation places the supremacy of eye as the most superior organ capable of comprehending the unity of experiences over all the other organs and devices. Thus, it strives to project the epiphenomena as the essence. In that case the dissolution of holism and the denigration of vision are considered as just different ways of describing the same process[20]. Thus, the totality of Nation rests on its ability to overcome the binary opposition between the subject and the object, identity and difference, autonomy and consent. This becomes the symbol of contradiction which is unfragmented and without conflicts. But, such an existence of totality in case of the Nation is implicitly utopian as it refuses to accept the other visions evolved through the personal experiences of various culture groups. Such an aspect of totality without accepting the heterotopias as real and living as any other similar entity, the claims of totality "the one and the indivisible" tends to degenerate into totalitarianism, homogenisation or regimentation. Such tendencies are always detrimental to the cause of human freedom including regards for human rights.

Nation as Universal Without a Universe

Flowing from the vision of totality, theoretically speaking Nation belongs to one and all without discrimination. And accordingly the nationalist philosophers claimed that Nation is a universal entity. It is applicable irrespective of the differences in the textually and contextually and time and space. The claims that evolution of diverse cultures, ethnic and identity groups into a National identity is a universal and transhistorical aspiration common to all, forms the core of the principle of universalism. The universality of this complex entity lies in non-antagonistically resolving most of the social contradictions ranging from modes of production, social formation, multi-culturalism etc., and amicably regressing these diversities into one or a few commonly accepted universal symbols—language, ideology, philosophy, economic life and governance by a non-partisan State[21]. Therefore, national symbols like national flag, currency, Constitution, national language, national religion, national dress, national festivals, national party etc, are not only valorized but, made mandatory to all citizens and the defaulters are penalised under the national law or penal code. The legitimacy of these claims gets further consolidated by assigning universal rights and universal franchise to the common masses for incorporating them under the hegemonic control of the sovereign power of the State within the Nation.

The claims of universality in the context of entity like Nation in which the culture, ethics and psychology of the people play the most fundamental role is possible only by reducing the masses to their existence. By restricting their mind within their body, nations have historically lived and progressed by suppressing principles of diversity and variations. Its claims of universal have been possible by annihilating the differences rather than accepting them. National spirit everywhere thrives on megalothymia *i.e.* a desire to be recognised better than other and to achieve this end which is both legitimate and rational. Thus, it has existed by alienating and marginalising the masses and any attempt to construct the universal under such circumstances is decided against the popular will of the people. The vision of totality degenerates into totalitarianism.

Nation as Instrumentally Rational

For presenting the vision of totality and universality it was important for the Nationalist scholars to standardise the production of knowledge. It was therefore an imperative to take recourse to certain epistemological measures of the production and distribution of new facts, logical system of truth, value system and the knowledge itself. Rationality from this standpoint means getting hold of some facts and accepting them as truth that have been proved valid through specific experimentation carried under specified technical arrangement and logical system. To become a truth of universal acceptance, validity and recognition, the experimental truth should be reproducible and should maintain consistency. In other words, to be rational under this purview means:—

To choose standards that must never be overruled by standard of a different kind meaning thereby, to maintain internal consistency and integrity at all costs and the standard must have heuristic force as well; that is the activity that is governed by them must be different from the intellectual freelancing of the anarchist.

Thus, rationality achieved under such arrangements does not mean finding better and humanistic truth but a truth that is repetitive, continuous and permanent. Most often, such a system of finding the truth is transmitted beyond the ruling power structure and it is carried by a group or community of people mostly in peer groups in pursuit of common interests. These groups converse in a language and symbol of their own that can be interpreted and demystified by using similar instruments[22]. In such a truth there is hardly any place for cultural and social aspects of truth. Infact, truth not only varies with change in the epistemological tools but the notion of Ontological relativism tends to alter the entire notion of truth itself meaning thereby truth is anything other than universal, rational and total. In fact, it is always a product of localised beliefs[23].

For Habermas the universality of reason hinges on formal or procedural concept of rationality owing much to the linguistic turn rather than the shift in the foundation itself. Reason merely externalises the subject by uprooting and tearing it from its cultural and social roots. This ultimately succeeds in the colonisation of the subject by the inversion of the externalities against the subject.

In the process of socialisation the intensity of differentiation gets ever sharpened and ultimately results in unique kind of network of relationship, which ultimately colonises the life world by the system, and communicative action by strategic action.

System comprising the economy and the State, formulates the rules of strategic action, controls the life world (comprising the public and the private spheres) and also controls the communicative action. When rationality of this nature once succeeds in becoming an instrument in the hands of the nationalists it degenerates into the ideology of the ruling class and is used then against the voice of difference and ultimately provides the much needed impetus to the dissolution of masses as living entity. A nation of this category then represents a naked display of barbarism.

Moreover to the nationalist philosophers, the project of nation formation was a process of linear progression based on the logical sequence of act-technology-experiment-truth-reason-universalisation and ultimately human freedom. The sole justification for all the experiences lay in the success of Nation in Europe and its subsequent empirical validation under certain technical scrutiny in other parts of the world and once it was proved valid for a particular situation then the same was recommended to other situations on the principles of rational and universal justification.

Since rationality is the sole justification for the existence of any substance, therefore Nation is also the epitome of ultimate rationality and all the other entities are considered as irrational, unnatural, unwanted and primordial. Thus, it was fundamental right of the Nation to incorporate and impose it's own self justifications on others particularly, those it considered as irrational. It is largely due to such a dogmatic understanding of rationality and use of political power in imposing it over the masses that have equated it with the ideology of the power elites. Thus, it has brought the concept of rationality itself within the arena of class struggle, which in the context of a nation will amount to fight against the Nationalist ideology by the ideologies of difference.

Nation as Modernity and Enlightenment

It was mentioned in the previous section that the projects of Modernity, Enlightenment and Rationality and the process of nation formation have their origin in one and the same processes active since late 18th to the 19th century. It was based on the use of reason, technocratisation and standardisation of human knowledge and production, along with beliefs etc, in a linear progress and universal nature of absolute truth[24]. The quintessence of its modernity lay in technical control of society over the forces of nature and supremacy of instrumental reason over the emancipatory or practical reason. Thus, displacement of deep ecology and intutitional rationality by occulacentric objectification had become the characteristic feature of the ethos of modernity with its philosophical foundations in the Enlightenment.

Enlightenment according to Kant is the self conscious intellectual movement for the emergence of man from self incurred immaturity to the realm of reason[25]. At the core of this crystallising project of modernity was his vindication of a concept of reason[26]. According to Habermas the project of modernity was formulated in the 18th century by the philosophers of the Enlightenment. It consisted of their efforts to develop objective science, universal morality, law and autonomous art etc., compatible to the inner logic of the Movement. And , at the same time the project also intended to release the cognitive potentials of each of these domains from their esoteric forms. But, unfortunately the project of modernity failed mainly on two counts namely: —

in honouring its promise most evidently concerning the rational construction of a good society, and,

by inverting the philosophical basis of freedom i.e. displacement of emancipatory reason by instrumental reason.

Thus, as long as the distorted concept of Modernity and Enlightenment continues to be the sole determining factor in the life of a Nation the realisation of human freedom can hardly be possible. Therefore, in spite of the saga of metanarratives supposedly offering the prospect of the emancipation of the epistemological and moral subject and the attainment of universal truth in science, morality and art etc., will degenerate into the fake jargons of authenticity. Under such pretensions it is certain that not only the unity and integrity of the individuals will always be illusive but, the realisation of ones creative potential will become increasingly more difficult.

Nation as (L)egality and (M)orality

The general and wider acceptance of Nation as a system of social functionalism is based on the principle of an ultimate legalising system of rules and regulations. The task of maintaining the legalistic and moralistic position of a Nation is carried through the ideological apparatuses of state. State with the help of these apparatuses succeeds in generating regular and voluntary consent among the masses much needed for the continuation of the Nation. Failure on the part of these apparatuses to perform their functions will not only undermine the bond of internal cohesion but it can also prove detrimental to their very existence including erosion in the sovereignty and political autonomy of the Nation. In case of failure of receiving regular consent through the organs of state ideological apparatuses the Nation activates the repressive organs of the state and use of political power and force becomes more blatant and coercive. Most often, it is done at the cost of democratic rights and civil liberties. As a consequence people experience abrupt erosion in limits of their choices. Sustained suspension of choices not only raise questions about the legitimacy of the Nation state but it also provides a basis for the emergence of counter hegemony against the hegemony of the Nation. It has been the common experience of the people of the world over that increasing dependence by the Nation-state on its repressive organs has been possible by inserting both legal and moral indignation on the masses.

Nation as Freedom?

Freedom stands for availability of choices, The success of Nation as an universally accepted entity rests on its ability in providing multiple choices before its citizens. It is largely due to this sense of ample choices that the citizens not only feel confident and secure within a Nation-State but they also receive psychological satisfaction in realising their full freedom including freedom of opportunity and creativity. This particular sense of freedom was mostly unheard of in earlier forms of social formations and nation has decidedly gained immensely due to this which is also considered vital from the point of human liberation. This is perhaps the most essential qualification for a Nation. According to J.S. Mill, Nation should be defined by the possession of a national sentiment along with the desire of the members of a nationality to be under the same government governed by themselves or a portion of themselves exclusively[26]. Here, government ability means the dissolution and decentring of power from the privileged ones to the general masses. Thus, freedom in the real sense means empowerment of the people. But unfortunately the history of modernity shows us that the power of the nation has been inversely related to the power of the masses. Therefore, so long as the Nation-State continues to remain the epitome of power and the omnipotent, the gamut of choices before the masses, will continue to be fewer and farther. And all the attempts on the part of the dissidents will be dealt firmly through the use of force.

Nation as Identity

The history before the rise of the modern Nation-State was infested with fuzzy[27] or overlapping of identities without any one being permanent in character and nature. It was for the first time after the emergence of the Nation-State that most of the fuzzy identities have been regressed into one or a few of the dominant identity formations and these have also become permanent in nature to a great extent. Here, the concept fuzzy does not mean that they had no clear identity of their own. On the contrary, it simply means that they had more than one identity at one and the same time. But the only difference was that the line of demarcation between one and the other identity was a matter of convenience rather than that of free choice. With the onset of modernity, standardisation of identities into one or a few universal identities has posed serious problems before the mankind as cultural being. Moreover, use of culture by the power elites to gain hegemonic control over the subaltern has also brought in the identity politics and culture within the ambit of power struggle. The Nation-States are increasingly becoming intolerant to the identity politics and subaltern cultures. In place of diverse popular cultures and identities, production of national culture and identity by the state owned culture industry has become their patent in the modern times.

National as Space

The concept of space is much older than human civilisation. It is said that animals too have territorial imperatives. But, upsurge of space consciousness among human beings in the modern times is worth noticing. According to Foucault "the present epoch will perhaps be the epoch of spaces"[28]. Roughly speaking the middle ages had hierarchic ensemble of spaces : the sacred, the profane, the protected, the open, the exposed, the urban, and the rural spaces etc, and all these were concerned with the real life experiences of human beings. Apart from this, every culture group had a cosmological theory of super celestial, celestial and terrestrial spaces. It was a space of complete hierarchy as opposed to a space of emplacement. It was a closed space. For the first time this, concept of space was shattered by Galileo in the mid 17th century and it was replaced by an infinitely open space in which the medieval space did not only get dissolved but also became merely a point and the extension got frozen into localisation. Today, this localisation has been further dissolved into relative space as opposed to absolute space. Space in relation to proximity, accessibility, technical feasibility etc, has greater practicability than its sacred aspects. But, more significantly due to relationship of propinquity *i.e.* what type of storage, circulation, making and classification of human beings, should be adopted in a given situation in order to achieve a given end space has only commer ' significance. Space in which we live today draws us out of ourselves in which the erosion of our lives, our time, our history occurs and is the space that claws and knows at use it is also the space which in real terms is a heterogeneous space[29]. We have private and public space, family: and social space, cultural and useful space, space of leisure and space of work etc., but, of all the spaces Nation is the most dominant one. And it is within this that all the other spaces are subsumed and get appropriated in the name of national integration and unity. With the upsurge in the movements for a return to the source, every culture group is also aspiring to gain control over its lost space and in its turn is increasingly becoming clear to the various dissident groups world over that the realization of human rights is impossible without its realisation in terms of independent space.

Thus, to conclude the forgoing discussion, it can be said that the concept of Nation and the philosophy behind it are both antithetical to human freedom. All that the Nation stands for has its roots in force and use of power rather than tolerance and compassion. Therefore, realisation of human and civil rights within the nationalised civilisation is paradoxical. Nation in the first and the last instance is power in absolute. The Leviathan represents an omnipotent and omnipresent armature of administrative power constantly vigilant and regimented, isolated and yet a self-policing subject member of a panoptic society.

NOTES AND REFERENCES

1. Karl Marx : *Economic and Philosophic Manuscript of 1844*, Progress Publishers, Moscow. 1977, p.71.
2. Albert Camus: *Resistance, Rebellian and Death,* Pergamon Press, New York, 1979, p.13.
3. Walter Bagehot : *Physic and Politics.* London 1887, pp. 20-1 as cited in *Nation and Nationalism Since 1780,* Eric J. Hobsbawm, Cambridge University Press, Canto Edition, Cambridge, 1994, pp. l. and 23.
4. Eric. Hobsbawm, *ibid.*, p.1.
5. Istvan Hont : "The Permanent Crisis of a Divided Mankind : Contemporary Crisis of the Nation State in Historical Perspective", *Political Studies,* Vol. 42. Special Issue, 1994, p.167.
6. John Dunn "Introduction : Crisis of Nation State?", *Political Studies, Ibid.*, p. 4.
7. V.L. Lenin, as quoted in. *Ibid.*, p. 1.
8. John Dunn *op. cit.*, p. 12.
9. Rajaram Dasgupta "Subsidies, Patents and Market Access in Dunkel Draft", *Economic and Political Weekly, May* 1, 1993, p. 855 and also in "Paradigm of Liberalisation : Compatibility with Social Concern?", Kamal Nayan, Kabra *The Indian Journal of Public Administration,* Vol. 42, No.3, 1996, pp. 270-83.
10. John Dunn *op.cit.*, p. 13.
11. Arjun Appadurai : *Modernity at Large : Cultural Dimensions of Globalisation,* University of Minnesota Press, 1996, p. 6.

12. *Ibid.*, p. 6.
13. *Ibid.*, pp. 9-19.
14. B.S. Butola : "The Myth of Ethnic-Nationalism", *Ethnicity, Culture and Nationalism in North-East India,* (Ed.) M.M. Agrawal, Indus Publishing Company, New Delhi, 1996, p. 126.
15. Peter Dews : " Power and Subjectivity in Foucault, *New Left Review,* No. 144, March-April, 1984, pp. 72-95.
16. E.J. Hobsbawm : *Nation and Nationalism Since 1780 Programme, Myth, Reality*, Cambridge University Press, 1994, p.18
17. *Ibid.*, pp. 18-9.
18. *Ibid.*, p. 20.
19. Jean Paul Sartre : *Critique of Dialectical Reason : Theory of Practical Ensemble*, New Left Books, Verso, London, 1982, p. 45.
20. Malcolm Bull: "Vision and Totality", *New Left Review,* p. 140.
21. Joseph Vladimir Stalin : *Problems of Leninism*, Foreign Language Press, Peking, 1976, pp. 67-77.
22. Paul Feyerabend, *Against Method : Outline of an Anarchistic Theory of Knowledge*, New Left Books, Verso, 1986, p. 196.
23. Christopher Norris : "Truth, Science and the Growth of Knowledge", *New Left Review*, No. 210, March-April, 1995, p. 109.
24. Ellen Meiksins Wood : "Modernity, Post-Modernity or Capitalism", *Monthly Review*, July-August, 1996, p. 23.
25. Graham Scambler : "The Project of Modernity and the Parameters for a Critical Sociology: An Argument with illustration from Medical Sociology", *Sociology*, Vol. 30, No. 3, August 1996, p. 568.
26. J.S. Mill : *Utilitarianism, Liberty and Representative Government,* Everyman Edition, London, 1910, pp. 359-66
27. Sudipta Kaviraj: "The Imaginary Institution of India", *Subaltern Studies*, Vol. VII, Oxford University Press, Delhi, pp. 1-39
28. Michel Foucault: "Of Other Spaces", *Diacritics,* Spring, 1986, pp. 22-7.
29. *Ibid.*, p. 23.

13

Rights Consciousness and the Other

*A 'Parapolitical' * Approach to Human Rights*

Goutam Biswas

I

The concept of Human Rights occupies an important segment of democratic thought transmitted from the European tradition to international affairs. It has undergone a process of formulation and reformulation, addition and alteration since the end of the Second World War. In principle,

> "it is a revival and extension of ideas associated with natural law in the seventeenth and eighteenth centuries under the name of 'natural rights' and then the 'rights of man'."[1]

They were considered to be natural because like natural law they did not depend upon man-made law. But with growing complexities in socio-historical, cultural, economic and political spheres of human life, human rights can no more be taken synonymously with natural law and natural rights. The scope of Human Rights, therefore, has been stretched beyond its earlier formulations. Cultural rights and gender rights, for example, are now integral components of Human Rights. With the entry of such concepts and theoretical constructions into the domain of human rights, the concept of Human Rights today bears an evolutionary landmark beyond naturalism and biologism—a landmark which signifies a transcendence towards a parapolitically envisioned

* Following Raghavan Iyer's explication 'Parapolities' is conceived here as a critique of conventional politics and not as something subordinate to politics.

goal of freedom through human participation in the world of Otherness. The world of Otherness is the dynamic world of extending self or selves,—extending beyond insularity and encapsulation to what the particular self is not. This is a transcendental evolution in the context of which Rights consciousness of human subjects undergoes a change and sends a feed-back to them demanding a fresh understanding of their Rights and a fresh stipulation of the concept of Rights within and outside themselves and/or their communities. But the parapolitical vision gets blurred and this transcendental evolutionary progress of the *anthropos* is arrested when Rights consciousness of human subjects as the basis of their self-assertion admist Others is overridden and the Otherness of such subjects is denied. At this juncture violation of Human Rights takes place and Rights consciousness receives a collective connotation in the context of such violation.

Violation of Human Rights occurs when Rights consciousness is monopolised by a dominant group to marginalise other groups or by a group attempting to hegemonise the entire cultural space.[2] A politics of tension remains ever alive in such a context, and it mars Human Rights. The situation becomes worse when the nation-state interferes with all its power machineries to subdue the tension for the sake of its administration and its ruling over a larger geographical and political territory. The ethics of such interference is then artificially grounded upon notions like *security* and *integrity,* and a justificatory logic to violate any norm and any Right is accrued from this baseless ethics.

Rights consciousness, therefore, requires an explication from the standpoint of parapolitics or politics of vision which would unhesitatingly recommend a social translation of this consciousness in terms of a recognition of *Swaraj* for every social, cultural and religious group and every individual within the group. Rights consciousness, in the true sense of the term, would thereby mean not only a basis of self-assertion but also assertion for the Other.

Insurgency in North-East India can be reviewed afresh against this normative and theoretical background, and the politics of tension can be countered from a parapolitical space for dialogue among diverse ethnic and cultural groups with the hope that the final victory shall be that of the latter. The positive role of Indian Nation-State in this context would be to shed off its *statism* and lend protection to the marginalised from annihilation and torture. Unfortunately, the story takes a different turn when the State itself plays a dominant role in the name of curbing and containing ethnic violence, and paradoxically, for the sake of its official philosophy of non-violence and tolerance. Consequent upon this, it adds a different dimension to the political scenario in North-East India under the head of *counter-insurgency.* While the attempt of contesting ethnic groups is to marginalise each other and the constructs of the politics of tension and politics of difference[3] remain confined to this attempt, the statist standpoint proposes to function as a larger body politics with a view to encompassing them all. The hollowness of the ethics of statism is obvious as it clings on to its own politics of power and politics of stability (for power) which are parapolitically insignificant. Parapolitics serves as a critical and evaluative standard to regenerate politics as an integral part of the transcendental evolution of the human towards freedom. It is necessitated by *that which ought not to be* in the sphere of politics, and it signifies also "the imaginative application of seminal ideas vitalising political theory and practice" and "quest for political understanding and action based upon expanding self-awareness".[4] A philosophical import of the concept of Human Rights can be sought by making an in-depth and critical study of some cases of serious violation of such Rights and in terms of a link between politics and parapolitics. I take North-East India as an example.

II

Marginalisation, indifference, resentment and hatred are the acute causes of the violation of Human Rights in the politically outstationed North-Eastern region of India. Both insurgency and counter-insurgency in North-East India have some justificatory logic from their respective standpoints which cannot get together as they do not have a sharable world-view and *telos.* The *telos* of insurgent outfits is to gain or restore their politics of self-preservation and homeostasis ensuring primarily the communitarian rights of people within the specific ethnic group. The *telos* of counter-insurgent forces is to bring the violent and rebel groups back to a national mainstream which for the retention of its multi-culturalist perspective, tends to diffuse the cultural specificities of these ethnic groups. Even to imagine a relational trust and consequently a confirmation of Otherness on the part of any of these two parties inclined to reject the other or to usurp the lead in the battlefield is a well-nigh impossibility. Rights consciousness, be it with the insurgents or counter-insurgents, has a clear collective connotation in this case and it is ostensibly divorced from the notion of the Other. Ironically, the fiftieth anniversary of the United Nations and UNESCO and the United Nations year for Tolerance was observed in 1995 and it was stressed that "only through a daily effort to know others better—I am the 'Other'!—and respect them that we would be able to tackle at source the problems of marginalization, indifference, resentment and hatred".[5] It was thereby thought to be "the only way to break the vicious circle that leads from insults to conforntation and the use of force".[6] In North-East India's perspective, the mutually contesting standpoints of not recognising the other as Other. Derecognition of the other relegates Rights consciousness to a hollow, repetitive monologue,—something like a Chatter Box which keeps on repeating '*Aham Brahmasmi*' ('I am that Brahman')!

The talk of fraternity, friendship, peace and harmony by the mainstream politicians is philosophically vacuous because it does not contain the spirit of genuine multi-culturalism which is like genuine multi-religionism of Shri Ramakrishna's kind. Politics in Indian mainstream shows interest in other cultures but does not honour their Otherness. With reference to celebrities like Gandhi, Tagore and Ambedkar, it paradoxically speaks for diversity, but masks and dilutes ethno-centric interests, values and *Weltanschauung*. Ultimately, it anchors the cultural politics to hierarchy of cultures and traditions. An Indian metropolis, for example, in spite of its cosmopolitanism, reflects the ethos of the dominant culture. This is how pseudo-multiculturalism is based on a subtle cunning of reason which prolifically vouches for rights of all cultures but under the umbrella of a mainstream politics. A not so far flung consequence of this hypocrisy is the construction of a political anthropology in a vacuity—an anthropology which tries to view the human without any root and in some so-called 'universalist' terms. Such an anthropology cannot take "forms" of representation in terms of depth-dimension and allegories in ethnographic texts seriously. In fact, it distorts the very interface between politics and anthropology.

The spirit of mainstream Indian politics resembles that of western liberal humanism in this respect. It maintains that "all people share essential human qualities and deserve respect and the opportunity to realise their full potential"[7] and it serves as an "important basis for concepts of universal Human Rights as espoused, for example, by the United Nations and innumerable organisations and pressure groups".[8] But it is observed that western Piberalism too suffers from certain serious contradictions:

"Despite the all-inclusive claims made for these rights, they mainly

> functioned, historically, on behalf of quite specific bourgeois, white, male interests. They have often privileged the wealthy at the expense of the poor, 'Man' at the expense of Woman, European interests at the expense of Others". [9]

Unlike western liberalism, Indian polity harbours some elements of feudalism in its coercive measures adopted for the sake of 'stability' and in the name of 'nationalism'. Examples of atrocities of partymen on innocent and free voters during elections are not very rare. Their justification lies in party-interest which is vindicated in the name of national interest. Use of private armies of landlords in some pockets of Bihar and Uttar Pradesh against landless poor and 'Dalits', rape of women, discriminatory measures against Scheduled Castes (men and women) are rampant and not infrequently under political protection. Alongside this, the severity and ruthlessness of Government-sponsored terrorism against insurgents and common people in insurgent areas cannot be expressed in words. They are even devoid of feudal benevolence and mercy. Some such cases were recorded during operation 'Rhino', 1991 in Assam. Let us read a few lines on 'Indiscriminate Mass Raids', as noted in *Human Rights: Principles, Practices and Abuses*:[10]

"Section 4(d) of the (Assam) Armed Forces Special Powers Act empowers Commissioned officer, warrant officer, NCO or any other person of equivalent rank in Armed Forces 'to enter' and search without warrant, any premises, to make any such arrests as aforesaid [*e.g.* any person who has committed a cognizable offence or against whom a reasonable suspicion exists that he has committed or is about to commit a cognizable offernce—S4(c)]. Under provision of this power, the army has started indiscriminate mass raids in thousands of villages. Not less than 4,000 villages (by a rough estimate from newspapers reports, Government press releases and actual on site reports) all over the state have been subjected to this form of search. The nature of such a mass raid is too horrendous even to describe....We would like to present a case study of such a raid...

The village concerned is called Bodhakora (P.O. Bodhakora, Mouza Kadom, Lakhimpur district). This is a large village containing various chubas as No. 1 Haridas No. 2 Haridas etc. It is a large village of mixed population inhabited by very poor people, mainly daily wage labourers and marginal farmers.

On 4th October, a large contingent of army (Rajputana Rifles) surrounded the village and conducted a house to house search. During house search, all male members were dragged out, some even from bed and were manhandled and beaten up at home itself. Womenfolk were abused. Some were slapped, some even hit by rifle and there were many cases of sexual molestation. Most of the male members, specially younger ones, (irrespective of age) were rounded up. They were taken to two interrogation camps, one situated in the field of the local school, another at about 2.5 km, away from the village inside a reserve forest at the bank of Ghagar river. Most of the men were beaten on way to these camps... the army jawans forced the men to carry them on their backs over a muddy and swampy area. Even when the jawans were riding their human horse they did not stop beating the men carrying them. The Major-in-charge of the operation rode on the back of a respected elderly teacher of the village.

In the camp areas, the people were humiliated and punished in various ways as given below:

— They were made to kneel down facing the sun;

— They were made to run in circles or do frog jumps till they fell down exhausted;...

During interrogations of the villages one after another, they were subjected to merciless beating with lathis, rifle butts and whips; many were kicked, punched and trampled on the ground. A few were stripped and electric shocks were applied to their body including private parts (genitalia). Hairs were pulled up. A few were crammed into a small cage and kept locked. The villagers describe the interrogation camp at the bank of Ghagar river as a virtual hell filled with the screams of the damned and shouts and abuses of the sadistic tormentors.

The most interesting point is that in this mass interrogation and raid, the army failed to catch a single hard-core insurgent. Most of the people rounded up were released by evening or night...It is very difficult to understand the logic of the useless raids, mass torture and interrogations unless the purpose is for the creation of pure terror for some sinister and ulterior motives."[10]

Army interrogation too is anything but a dialogue. It bears the typical power to annihilate the other from the very beginning. In fact, as Sartre pointed out, interrogation of any nature expresses the possibility of non-being. Army interrogation and interrogation in police custody prove this so glaringly that it does not simply express the 'possibility' but it actually terrorises the other to such an extent that he/she loses his/her being and becomes a ghostly shadow with fear and trembling, tottering on the brink of nothingness. It is horrible even to know the methods of torture adopted by Army and paramilitary forces during interrogations.

Methods of interrogation and torture are gristly.....most of the times, people were not interrogated properly, but nevertheless tortured. Torture acquires an independent existence—a momentum of its own and a sadistic sinister underpinning. This makes it a tool for creating pure terror. The methods used so far are as follows:[11]

— "Beating: both in public view, at home before family members and also inside the camps by hands, lathis, rifle, butts, whips.
— Punching in face, head, abdomen.
— Trampling and kicking a man, made to lie down on ground.
— Beating with lathis on soles of feet.
— Hanging: Hanging the person from ceiling beam; by hands.
— Hanging from tree, in upside down position.
— Hanging a person by one hand only....
After a person is so hanged, he is severely beaten...
— Wet Submarine treatment: Immersing the head of the person in a basket or drum of water till he is nearly drowned.
— Continuously pouring water over the mouth and nose of a person after he is bound up and immobilised in ground till he is nearly suffocated...
— Frame Treatment: A person is bound spread-eagled to a vertical rectangular wooden frame and thus immoblised, one is tortured.
— Giving Electric Shock: Electric shock is given from a 12 Volt car battery directly from domestic mains. Shocks are given to head, eyes, cheeks, ears, neck, shoulders, armpits, back and even to private parts.
— Uprooting hairs by pincers from head, eyebrow, armpit and even pubic hair.
— Hitting a person on his genitalia and testes till he becomes unconscious from pain.
— Applying chilli powder to eyes and also to anus.
— Forcefully pulling apart the legs by two soldiers.
— Pushing a stout lathi smeared with chilli powder and petrol through the anus.
— Burning with lighted cigarette butts. Such burns are even given to private parts.

— Sticking pins all over the body.

— Burying in ground upto neck and covering the head with a bucket.

— Denying food and water for days together.

General physical punishment and humiliation. Usually large groups are subjected to these. People are lined up in a field or in camps, sometimes in full view of the womenfolk and are forced to do the following.

a) To kneel facing the sun for hours,

b) To stand naked in sun and rain,

c) To stand in waistdeep or neckdeep water for hours,

c) To perform frog jumps till the person is exhausted,

e) To run in circles.

f) To carry army jawans on back over long distances,

g) To perform sit ups holding the ears,

h) Forcing to eat sand, earth or to drink alcohol and filthy water.

During all these procedures the army uses filthy and abusive language. Most of the times, specifically during night time the army jawans are mostly drunk.

During raids and searches, army jawans usually misbehave with the women. At the slighest pretext they lay hands on women, pull them by hand, pull away their clothes, sometimes actually strip them naked; molestation and attempted molestation are occurring everyday...

A heinous incident of confining two women to their homes and repeatedly raping them every night by army jawans have also come to light and is reported.

All the blood curdling modalities of torture listed above are tabulated from actual interviews and signed statements of the victims. Many other methods of torture that have been used are not tabulated here because such statements are not at hand....

During such interrogation the victims are strictly always blindfolded so that afterwards they cannot identify their tormentors.

The most disturbing features of the widespread inhuman torture are as follows:

1. Persons tortured are losing their mental balance, suffering from severe insomnia and are becoming paranoid.
2. Those given electric shocks to the head are suffering from intense headache, memory lapses, inco-ordination of thought and action, visual disturbances....

3. Those who are physically tortured, specially those who are kicked, trampled upon or beaten with lathis are having:
   — Severe muscle and joint pains,
   — Blood vomiting,
   — Passage of blood in urine,
   — Inability to use one or more arms, forearms, fingers, legs, etc.
   — Damaged reflexes and other neurological features.
4. Those who have been tortured in genitalia are developing loss of libido, impotence and other sexual abnormalities".[11]

The United Nations considers rights of humans as integral parts of human nature. Neither insurgency nor counter-insurgency can ensure such rights for the people because in both the approaches human nature is either degraded or perverted. Operations of insurgent outfits often exhibit the dominance of a collective ego, an absolutely community-based approach to human reality and thereby a de-recognition of others in and outside the community. This has sociological, political and economic reasons. Such reasons are vaguely conjectured and very often manifest (not systematically) when the insurgents of North-East India conceptualise their relation with the State or the mainstream politics as an unequal one, or as that between the 'coloniser' and the 'colonised'. Hence, the possibility to theorise their status for a positive solution cannot be altogether ruled out in a federal framework. The moral philosophical degradation can be checked by the people of the communities themselves when the causes of insurgency are removed. In a contrary manner, operations of counter-insurgent forces (as described above) do not reflect the slightest proximity or affinity with human nature. In their methods of interrogation and torture and by their whims during mass raids, human rights are violated straightaway. Far from speaking of human nature, they deny the minimum existential and subjective status to human 'body'. A human body, for them, is not an 'Other'. A human body, for them, is a *being-in-itself or en soi.* The point, therefore, is to suspend their political and nationalistic underpinning, and initiate a parapolitical review of contemporary politics of power.

III

"Parapolitics', as Raghavan Iyer puts it, "involves continuous rethinking of the foundations as well as the frontiers of conventional politics".[12]

Whereas the format of contemporary politics incorporates the idea of human rights and its allied ideas as its part and parcel, abuse and violation of such rights forms the problematic of the literature on contemporary politics. It is not that the rights of humans were never violated in the past. But now various facets and multifarious layers of the meaning of the idea of human rights are explored and taken notice of in the context of the complexities of socio-historical and cultural panorama,—the complexities which history did not witness earlier to this extent. Though the conventional politics in the so-called geographical and socio-cultural mainstream of India today cannot afford to ignore this fact, it is transparent to anybody that this politics is ugly and bereft of any right to speak of human rights. This is a parapolitical assertion voiced by many sensible Indian milieus. The literature on politics today cannot but accept it. Perhaps an ideal *Civitas Humana* or an ideal society of humans can never be slurred over in silence in any *polis,* and Rights consciousness of humans must be given expression in consonance with that ideal. Today the concept of Human Rights suffers from hermeneutic ambivalence because there are many such ideals the political legacy of which cannot be settled in the present framework without a decisive turn from both the past and the present for a spontaneous and critical evaluation of these ideals by people themselves. This standard must be open-ended and potent enough to cross the boundaries of Politics of Stability, Politics of Power and Politics of Self-Preservation. In any of these frameworks Otherness cannot emerge with its full significance. On the contrary, Otherness of Communities besides one's own will remain under perpetual domination and Otherness of individuals will be subjugated to the collectivity. Without Otherness Rights consciousness and Human Rights are of no value.

Politics of Stability and Politics of Power contain an innate inadequacy and incapability for a transcendence towards a Politics of Vision which characterises parapolitics. As Iyer points out, Politics of Stability "relies on the available means of coercion, conciliation and co-existence, and stresses the Logic of Contraction...The degrees of stability sought may vary, but....stability in a dynamic universe is an elusive goal,....Politics of Power, with its reliance on manipulation, propaganda, and persuasion, tends to pursue the Logic of Expansion through short-sighted methods of Political action".[13] Iyer rejects Politics of Self-Preservation too as it is "pre-occupied with the Logic of Equilibrium and a search for homeostasis", and "marked by deficiency of imagination".[14] But he was perhaps oblivious of the fact that Politics of Self-Preservation arises out of a more primitive scare of insecurity. A gradual freedom from this basic scare is possible when the organisational requirements of this politics are more or less fulfilled to ensure the right for self-preservation at the communitarian and individual levels. Such a possibility as latent in this politics resolves the paradox that notwithstanding the deficiency of imagination this politics, as Iyer himself admits, sometimes reveals itself with "sporadic exemplifications of a worldly wisdom that echoes higher possibilities".[15]

The Politics of Self-Preservation is based on the Rights consciousness of a community and individuals within it. But this consciousness remains unrefined, rudimentary and non-dynamic so long as the boundary of this politics is not questioned. A transcendental evolution of this consciousness bringing about the Politics of Perfectibility, Politics of Reason, and Politics of Welfare within its fold and finally linking itself vertically with the Politics of Vision is inevitable because all human societies have historically proved themselves as carriers of a *Surplus*—the *Surplus* expressed in achievements beyond smaller needs and need-based innovations and in self-perception beyond one's habitual territories of thought and action with a homogeneous and linear orientation to the Other. At this stage, the concept of Rights consciousness is nuanced afresh with reference to the Other.

For the promotion of Human Rights, the first move of a Government should be to let such evolution of a people take place and to provide all infrastructure for a pedagogic exercise to quicken the process of this evolution. The political will of a Government in a country like India which is multi-ethnic, multi-lingual and multi-religious should be para-politically tuned towards an idea of non-interference and non-imposition so that the ideas of development can emerge from within the particular ethnic communities as contributive to the *becoming of a larger nation* as distinguished from *nation at large.*

IV

Nation at large consists in a teleology of 'form'—a 'form' which is stable and permanent. It signifies a power legacy or authority over all distinct and unique ethno-cultural groups and individuals. In accordance with this teleology *one* history of *one* nation is written. This is *nation in the state of being* with an ontology concocted by and for the state attached to it. A single nationalism is propounded and vindicated on the basis of this ontology. Such a nationalism turns out to be an equivalent of Statism. In Indian political scenario, nationalism equated with Statism is the result of a cunning subversion of the theory of a *larger nation* or *nation in the state of becoming*. The concept of *larger nation* is to be distinguished from the concept of *nation at large*. The concept of *larger nation* signifies a dynamic process wherein participation from all communities and sections contributes to the formation of nation. There is no fixed teleology of form in this context. It is an endless process, *larger nation* is thus *nation in the state of becoming*, and it suits best the cultural reality of Indian subcontinent. As Sudipta Kaviraj points out.

> "if the nation-state had to be culturally homogeneous by definition, it did not fit the cultural reality of the Indian sub-continent: and one of the central divisions within nationalist ideology was between homogenizing and a pluralist trend. Nation-hood, the first view held, gave strength because it was great force of homogeneity and identity. But the more dominant and persuasive stands in Indian nationalism opposed this construction, and interestingly, Gandhi and Nehru were one in upholding a distinctively pluralist idea of the Indian nation though their detailed constructions were vastly different."[16]

This pluralistic idea of Indian nation-state is quite in consonance with Indian culture and society. But unfortunately, the homogenizing force in nationalist ideology has percolated into all branches of politics today. Those who uphold the pluralistic view are unfit to resolve the contradiction between the need for oneness and the retention of the pluralistic view of Indian society. As a result the idea of a single nationalism still prevails in the mainstream Indian politics. Violation of human rights by police, military and paramilitary forces can be easily traced to the state which asserts certain rights for a nationalistic *telos* and for the interest of *nation at large*. But such rights are not ontological to nation or nation-state conceived in this sense.

Nations and states or nation-states in their hyphenated existence do not have any right by themselves. It is the rights of humans which lend to nations and states whatever rights the later can be properly accorded. As John Dunn has correctly pointed out, rights of nations and states as 'products of power' do not have any 'ethical authority'.[17] He says,

> "The handbooks or official proclamations....from Samuel Pufendorf's

> Seventeenth Century De officio Hominis et Civics through the American Declaration of Independence of 1776 and the French Declaration of the Rights of Man and of the Citizen of 1789 to the United Nations Charter of our own day are intractably universalist. All of them take individual human beings, more or less as they are, as their fundamental ethical units and assess the legitimacy of possible laws or political arrangements in terms of axiomatically identical rights which such human beings are presumed to process."[18]

The Charter of Human Rights makes us aware of a trans-national and parapolitical perspective of human solidarity which the politics of our day needs for its own orientation. The idea of a single nationalism is based upon the concept of *nation at large.* A continuous deification of 'national interest', 'nationalism' and a 'single nation' from the standpoint of *nation at large* has ostensibly reduced the primacy of groups, (ethnic, linguistic, religious), group–values, value of communitarian and ethnological understanding for envisaging a *real* national space *i.e.* the larger nation or *nation in the state of becoming.* The more the deification of a single nationalism is spread by the state media and national integration is propagated, politics loses its subjective link with society, culture and values of people; it gets reified to an extreme. Nationalism thereby becomes a "habit of accommodation" of which we feel moral shabbiness readily enough ourselves."[19]

Integration is basically a cultural phenomenon preceded by natural convergence of ideas through social and productive purposes. It may serve politics, but it is not a political concept *per se.* Integration of ethno-cultural communities has become problematic in India because this fact of convergence of ideas and provision for such convergence in terms of education health care and communication are overlooked. Instead, slogans for integration have become more frequent against the backdrop of 'nationalism' and 'nationhood'. The futility of such efforts was foreseen by Rabindranath Tagore. He said,

> "....from the earliest beginnings of history India has had her own problem constantly before her—it is the race problem. Each nation must be conscious of its mission, and we in India must realise that we cut a poor figure when we try to be political, simply because we have not yet been finally able to accomplish what was set before us by our providence......The problem is whether different groups of peoples shall go on fighting with one another or find some true basis of reconciliation and mutual help...in my country we have been seeking to find out something common to all races, which will prove their real unity. No nation looking for a mere political or commercial basis *of unity will find such a solution sufficient*

....India has never had a real sense of nationalism. Even though from childhood I had been taught that idolatry of Nation is almost better than reverence for God and humanity, I believe I have outgrown that teaching, and it is my conviction that my countrymen will truly gain their India by fighting against the education which teaches them that a country is greater than the ideals of humanity."[20]

It is clear that Rights consciousness, with the loss of the ideals of humanity, cannot have any meaning. Nationalism based upon a fixed ontology and teleology must be rejected as the 'starkest political shame' and detrimental to the process of translating the charter of human rights into a socio-cultural reality for constructing the *Civitas Humana.*

V

I think the Gandhian concept of *Swaraj* of self-government can serve as a key principle, in a parapolitical and ethico-political sense, for envisioning a world of humans with full awareness of communitarian and individual rights corroborated by critical and interpretative competence of individual human beings. The Other in the Community or the Community as an Other to another Community cannot be dissolved, rejected or annihilated. This is the essence of the philosophy of *Swaraj.* The logic of *Swaraj* always creates a space for the Other and bears the possibility of an inter-cultural communication. The *Swaraj* of one cannot last through a negation of it for the Other. Ethnic violences and the statist approach to contain such violences through violent means are in clear opposition to this philosophy of *Swaraj.*

As the chief proponent of the philosophy of *Swaraj,* Gandhi clearly denounced a one-way authority of the national government over people for bringing about *Swaraj* among people. As *Swaraj* means also self-government with freedom for self-expression, Gandhi held that it is not a *thing* which can be given or taken away by anybody. Gandhi insisted upon a clear correspondence between individual *Swaraj* and national *Swaraj,* but, at the same time he maintained that the concept of individual *Swaraj* is logically and conceptually prior to national or collective *Swaraj.* He said,

"....after-all self -government depends entirely on our internal strength, upon our ability to fight against the heaviest odds. Indeed self-government which does not require that continuous striving to attain it and to sustain it is not worth the name. I have therefore endeavoured to show both in word and in deed, that self-government—that is self-government for a large number of men and women—is no better than individual self-government, and therefore, it is to be attained by precisely the same means that are required for individual self-government or self-rule, and so, as you know, I have striven in India to place this idea before the people in season and out of season, very often much to the disgust of those who are politically minded merely."[21]

Swaraj in individual's thought and action reflects its strict moral core in not defying the possibility of it with Others. As *Swaraj* involves a continuous striving both at individual and collective or national levels, no ontologically fixed concept of 'nation' can be entertained within its purview. On the contrary, it is the concept of *nation in the state of becoming or larger nation* as distinguished from the concept of *nation at large or nation in the state of being* which is in true consonance with the philosophy of *Swaraj*. The Gandhian perspective endorses *Swaraj*, in the true sense of the term, as a natural human right. Rights consciousness based upon *Swaraj* incorporates the Other and assigns all possible human rights to the Other. From this point of view Rights consciousness of humans is steeped in righteousness. There is no place of violence in this regard. This is true with respect to individuals and the community of individuals which should ideally be a *community of Others*. The balance between individual consciousness and collective consciousness is to be realised in terms of free exercise of the powers of humans to interpret, criticise communicate.

The ethics of non-violence underlying the concept of *Swaraj* is further legitimized by Gandhi's philosophical anthropology which makes a sharp distinction between humans and brutes. To be human, for Gandhi, is to cease to be bestial or brutal, and non-violence is the law of human species as violence is the law of the brute. This ethics and the philosophical anthropological assertion had a considerable impact upon Gandhi's political programme the merits and demerits of which, however, are worthy of discussion and analysis but in a different context. But the phenomena of present ethnic bifurcation, insurgency and counter-insurgency clearly show that the concept of *Swaraj* still awaits its due place in the format of contemporary political practice.

In today's context, *Swaraj* needs a praxiological orientation. It does not prescribe a passive and neutralistic acceptance of Others or an arrogant assertion of self—collective or individual self. It speaks of a practice at the interhuman and intercultural level. This practice is dialogical as opposed to a monological and hegemonic one. "Valuing the plurality of cultures and languages and the subtle ecological variety and nuance of human practice"[22] which Herder dreamt of can become a reality with *Swaraj* as a self-conscious project on the part of political institutions, social organisations and individuals. *In its praxiological sense, Swaraj implies a non-violent means (as the internal logic of the concept demands so) to assign agency to all socio-cultural and religious groups and dissolves the majoritarian and hegemonic perspective by invoking the dialogical relationship among diverse ethno-cultural groups and individuals so that all communities may transcend their conservatism to appropriate themselves for democratic politics in the context of a larger nation.*

The concept of Human Rights, therefore, demands a fresh heed from the standpoint of *Swaraj.* It does not propagate the possibility of an unrestrained pursuit of individual self-interest on the ground of distinctness, insularity and a cultivated indifference of one to the other. Nor does it propose an absolute collectivism or relativism in ethics. It involves social responsibility. *The concept of Human Rights, according to the philosophy of Swaraj, consists in Rights consciousness in conjunction with righteousness, recognition of and respect for the Other; it involves respectful, critical and interpretative understanding of the plurality of truth prevailing in diverse communities and the convergence of such truths through dialogue among moral equals.*

As rights of humans are universal, they imply universal ethical standards. But with the specific philosophical nuances of the concept of *Swaraj* added to such standards, their universality does not exclude the possibility of particular constructions of morality in terms of the infinite heterogeneity of discursive practices. A balance between the two is conceivable through the praxiology of *Swaraj* and its guiding force in all spheres of human social dynamics.

The Charter of Human Rights in the context of India and the entire Indian sub-continent receives a new significance from this standpoint. The rich experiential background of almost all the communities within it offers an ideal perspective to us, not for insurgency and counter-insurgency, but for traversing along multiple discourses scattered all over its map. It results in a continuous hermeneutical regeneration of Philosophy, Politics and Culture towards the conception of a trans-national federal framework and the creation of a *Cvitas Humana.*

NOTES AND REFERENCES

1. D.D. Raphael : *Problems of Political Philosophy*, Macmillan Press Ltd, 2nd edition, 1990, p. 104.
2. Cultural space is produced out of intersection of various unique modalities of producing oneself/selves and it acquires an original meaning in the context of the everyday life of a people.
3. Politics of difference consists in highlighting the indigenous, distinct and conservative character of a community and identifying all its socio-political programmes in terms of this character. Politics of tension arises out of insistence upon the autonomy and primacy of one community over others and a total subjugation of individual's life to a collective ego.
4. Raghavan Iyer. *Parapolitics: Toward the City of Man,* Concord Grove Press, USA, 1986, p. 27.
5. Federico Mayor. The Human Right to Peace: Declaration by the ' Director General', UNESCO, 1997.
6. *Ibid.*
7. Glenn Jordan & Chris Weedon (ed). *Cultural Politics: Class, Gender, Race and Postmodern World,* Blackwell, 1995, p. 29.
8. *Ibid.*, p. 29.
9. *Ibid.*, p. 24.
10. N. Sanajaoba (ed). *Human Rights: Principles, Practices & Abuses,* Omsons Publications, New Delhi, 1994, pp. 139-141.
11. *Ibid.*, pp. 142-146.
12. Raghavan Iyer, *op. cit.*, p. 1.
13. *Ibid.*, p. 25.
14. *Ibid.*, p. 27.
15. *Ibid.*, p. 27.
16. Sudipta Kabiraj. 'Crisis of the Nation-State in India', in John Dunn (ed) *Contemporary Crisis of the Nation State,* Blackwell, 1995, p. 119.
17. John Dunn. *Western Political Theory in the Face of the Future,* Cambridge University Press, Canto edition, 1993, p. 59.
18. *Ibid.*, p. 59.
19. *Ibid.*, p. 59.
20. Rabindranath Tagore : *Nationalism,* Rupa & Co., 1994, pp.77-78, 79-83.
21. M.K. Gandhi : *Young India,* December, 1927.
22. John Dunn, *op cit.*, p. 78.

Contributors

1. S.N. Bhargava : Chairperson State Human Rights Commission, Guahati., Assam.
2. Ranju R. Dhamala : Professor Deptt. of Political Science, Assam University, Silchar, Assam.
3. N. B. Biswas : Reader, Deptt. of Education, Assam University, Silchar, Assam.
4. Trigunesh Mukherjee : Former Commandant, Counter Insurgency Jungle Warfare School, Vairangte, Mizoram.
5. Abhik Gupta : Reader, Deptt. of Ecology, Assam University, Silchar, Assam.
6. Sajal Nag : Reader, Deptt. of History, Assam University, Silchar, Assam.
7. Chinmoy Kanti : Sr. Lecturer, Deptt. of Anthropology, G.C. College, Silchar.
8. Tanmoy Bhattacharjee : Reader, Deptt. of Political Science, Assam University, Silchar, Assam
9. Rajesh Dev : Lecturer, Deptt. of Political Science, Women's College, Shillong, Meghalaya.
10. Sukalpa Bhattacharjee : Lecturer, Deptt. of English, G.C. College, Silchar, Assam.
11. Prasenjit Biswas : Lecturer, Deptt. of Humanities & Social Sciences, Indian School of Mines, Dhanbad, Bihar. Currently Senior Lecturer at HSS Dept. IIT, Bombay
12. B.S. Butola : Reader, Deptt. of Geography, NEHU, Shillong. Currently, Reader, CSRD, JNU, New Delhi.
13. Goutam Biswas : Professor, Deptt. of Philosphy, Assam University, Silchar, Assam.